# White News

## Why Local News Programs Don't Cover People of Color

## LEA's Communication Series
### Jennings Bryant/Dolf Zillmann, General Editors

Selected titles in Journalism (Maxwell McCombs, Advisory Editor) include:

For a complete list of other titles in LEA's Communication Series, please contact Lawrence Erlbaum Associates, Publishers

# White News

## Why Local News Programs Don't Cover People of Color

## Don Heider
*University of Texas at Austin*

**LEA** LAWRENCE ERLBAUM ASSOCIATES, PUBLISHERS
2000  Mahwah, New Jersey                     London

Lawrence Erlbaum Associates, Inc., Publishers
10 Industrial Avenue
Mahwah, New Jersey 07430-2262

Library of Congress Cataloging-in-Publication Data


Heider, Don (Donald Bruce)
    White news : why local news programs don't cover people
of color / Don Heider.
        p.   cm.
    Includes bibliographical references and index.
    ISBN 0-8058-3475-3 (acid-free paper)
    1. Minorities—Press coverage—United States.
2. Television broadcasting of news—Hawaii—Honolulu. 3. Television broadcasting of news—New Mexico—Albuquerque. I. Title.
PN4888.M56 H45 2000
070.4'4930556'0973—dc21                          99-059207
                                                      CIP

Books published by Lawrence Erlbaum Associates are printed
on acid-free paper, and their bindings are chosen for strength
and durability


Printed in the United States of America
10  9  8  7  6  5  4  3  2  1

*To Jeanne, Anna, & Ella*
*and Geraldine Heider.*

*And let us consider how we may*
*spur one another on toward love and good deeds.*
*Hebrews 10:24*

# Contents

# Acknowledgments

Although my name appears on the cover, what is between the covers is the result of help from a number of different people.

While at the University of Colorado, Kathryn Rios inspired me to be a tough-minded scholar, but also encouraged me through her compassion, friendship and kindness. Lane Hirabayashi and Bob Trager provided consistently helpful and detailed constructive feedback. Maria Montoya, Tony DeFalco, Dennis McGilvray, David Stannard, Stewart Hoover, Patricia Adler and Shu-Ling Everett provided intellectual nourishment. Len Ackland provided weekly exercise for my psyche and for my body. Dave Martinez was always there to lend a hand … or an ear.

At Texas, cohorts Craig Watkins, Gigi Durham, Chuck Whitney, and Frank Durham have been excellent sounding boards and provided invaluable advice. Many of the faculty in journalism at the University of Texas help create an atmosphere where thinking and creating can flourish under leadership from Steve Reese.

Linda Bathgate at Lawrence Erlbaum Associates has been nothing but a joy to work with. Thanks to Robyn Goodman for her creativity and good eye in helping to design a book cover. Bill Davie at the University of Louisiana, Lafayette and Jim Upshaw at the University of Oregon provided some late inning relief help.

Reviewers have also helped strengthen the project and I owe them a debt of gratitude, especially Max McCombs. Other scholars' work that was influential along the way include the writings of Howard Winant, Robert Entman, and Christopher Campbell.

Jeanne Heider, my best friend, my wife, and partner read innumerable drafts and provided the eye of a good copy editor. As well, she tolerated all the time away and work that went into gathering research material. She at times encouraged, threatened, and cajoled me into finishing and meeting deadlines.

This research also would not have been possible without aid from the East-West Center, CU honors students who worked with me transcribing interviews, journalists who welcomed me into their newsrooms, and community leaders who were willing to take the time to offer their views.

# Introduction

At 5 p.m. turn on your television set. Click over until you find the local newscast. What do you see? Newscasters, likely on a handsome set, reading stories, accentuated by modern graphics and lots of videotape clips.

What may be more important is what you don't see. For among the newscasters, the experts, and the newsmakers you only occasionally will see a face that's not pink. Although I worked in television news for nearly 10 years, this is a fact that somehow escaped me until I quit the business and had the time and inclination to begin looking back on the business of which I had been a part, and even at the work I had myself done. I am White. For Anglo-Americans, color, especially the color white (or pink), is most often not noticed. We live in a country where millions of people can still go through their daily existence and never notice how Whites are in so many places, in so many authoritative positions, because it has been for so long the norm.

I was in Hawai'i in 1992, and as a former broadcast journalist, I wanted to see the local news. What I noticed about Hawai'i was that it was a unique place, probably one of the most unique of the United States. Not all that many pink people. The news came on. It was not unique. Except for the fact that I saw an occasional Hawaiian shirt, it reminded me of news in other U.S. cities. I could have been in Toledo, Ohio, or Syracuse, New York. How could that be, I wondered?

What I knew well from years of being in the news business was that local news is supposed to be somehow reflective of the local community. That was, at least, what I had believed and thought I had practiced during my career. Yet here was undeniable evidence to the contrary. That's where this book began, in a hotel room in Hawai'i.

When I began reading about race and news, I found that others had made the same observation, but in a more systematic way. There was a consensus, of sorts, that coverage of people of color, of communities of color was lacking. Yet having spent many mornings and afternoons sitting in on editorial meetings where news coverage decisions are made, I knew that journalists didn't generally sit around the table and say: "how can we exclude ————— (insert: Blacks, Latinos, Asians or Native Americans) today?" Yet if you watched our 5 p.m. show, it was as if that is *exactly* what we had done. So between 9 a.m., when most newsroom employees show up, and 5 or 6 p.m., when the day's primary newscast airs, what goes wrong? Doing an analysis of news program content could never fully answer that question. So I set about to take a more anthropological approach. I decided to go back into newsrooms, this time not as a journalist but as a researcher and observer. Unlike anthropological ethnographers who go to completely foreign settings and spend years living among villagers, I would go back to a place with which I was very familiar, but with a new perspective. My familiarity with the setting would give me an advantage, because I already understood how the system worked, how the villagers dressed, and talked, and behaved. I spoke the language. I knew the terrain. What's more, although I disclosed from the outset to news workers that I was coming into their workplace to study race and news, the fact that I was White, I believe, gave me a sense of discreteness. Newsrooms, despite what some may believe, are still hugely populated by Anglos, and that especially holds true when it comes to those in decision-making positions. Thus, as a White male or "one of them," I believe I was less threatening. As is seen here, people spoke to me quite frankly about race and news.

I went into two different newsrooms. I sat in on editorial meetings, I observed newsroom interactions, I went out on stories with reporters and photographers, and I shared meals with news workers and news managers. I had full access to the building, the newsroom computer system, all newsroom-wide memos, and all editorial meetings. In addition to observing what was going on, I conducted a number of in-depth interviews with newsroom employees. I interviewed photographers, videotape editors, reporters, assignment editors, producers, anchors, and news managers.

When it comes to news coverage, the newsroom is only part of the picture. To better understand how a news organization was or was not covering a particular community, it seemed to me I had to ask for input from that community. So I also spent time trying to identify and interview community leaders, all of whom were people of color. I spoke with state lawmakers, mayors, business owners, priests, tribal officials, and grassroots organizers. I gave them an opportunity to critique local news coverage. These interviews were particularly beneficial. These individuals, most of whom had never had the opportunity to speak out about coverage, had quite a bit to say about local news media. My primary criteria for finding these people was that they needed to be regular consumers of local news and were in some type of leadership role in their community. Those interviews make up a large part of the analysis that follows.

I spent a good deal of time thinking about the communities I would study. I decided from the outset to travel to cities where there was a large minority population. I also decided to select communities where African Americans were not the dominant minority group. I did this because the research that has been done on race and on race and media, too often frames questions in terms of Black and White. There is still much research to be done on how Black and White Americans do and do not interact, but for this study I decided to focus instead on other groups of people who are often left unstudied. I also wanted to select two cities that shared some common characteristics, so I could compare the information collected in each locale. This led me to Honolulu, Hawai'i and Albuquerque, New Mexico. Honolulu and Albuquerque both are medium-sized television markets, and both have large populations of people of color. In both places, the television stations cover virtually the entire state. Hawai'i was a sovereign country that, through military force, America took control of, then invited into statehood. New Mexico was a territory, which again, through military engagement, the United States acquired. In that way, both New Mexico and Hawai'i could be considered colonized territories. At the time of the study, New Mexico's population was about 51% White (though these figures have been disputed as being too high). In Hawai'i, there is no racial-ethnic majority.

A much more extensive discussion of the methodology for this study is included in the appendix.

Before I go further, it is important to clarify my own position, theoretical and otherwise, so readers have a better understanding of what ideas inform and influence me as a researcher. I clearly identify my thoughts about race as a social construct, and then briefly discuss what theories have influenced my view of the world.

## RACE AND ETHNICITY

Dictionary definitions of words such as *race* or *ethnicity* do not get us very far when it comes to gaining an understanding of the concepts behind those terms. For in this American culture, these terms can be complex and emotionally charged.

*Race* is a word that has been used for hundreds of years. In the development of European thought, the term became known as a way of identifying different typologies of human beings. In the early 1700s, Carolus Linnaeus, a Swedish botanist, offered an initial four-group classification of people. He was followed over the next several centuries by a myriad of others, from Kant to Blumenbach, who all offered their own taxonomies. Using geography, language, customs, and other variables, dozens of anthropologists and others attempted to devise successfully a scheme that would explain the differences between racial groups. From a biological and anthropological perspective, it seems the term *race* is meaningless if it is used in an effort to differentiate between one human and another, as it is impossible to make scientifically meaningful separations between different groups of humans. Even if one tries to construct ideal types within groups, the amount of biological and social diversity that occurs within groups makes this type of construction futile and ultimately absurd. According to the *Harvard Encyclopedia of American Ethnic*

*Groups* (1980): "[T]here is no single authoritative or scientific answer to the question of what are the races of mankind" (p. 869). Although biology and physical anthropology and a host of other disciplines ultimately have not been able to provide cogent scientific definitions for race or essentialized racial types, that does not mean a socially constructed idea of race does not exist. Indeed, the ideas that science has presented in regard to race have not been simply dismissed as they were disproved; many still remain as powerful and influential beliefs. It is remarkable to think that although ideas such as social Darwinism or a biological hierarchy of races have been disproved or dismissed, people still cling tightly to them. These ideas are finding support not only among those who use such ideas to oppress, but also among those who are oppressed. What this means is that no matter the lack of empirical underpinning a concept such as *race* may have, it remains important. Kwame Anthony Appiah (1995) said it this way:

> But, of course, a discussion of the … ramifications of the idea of race can proceed while accepting the essential unreality of races and the falsehood of most of what is believed about them. For, at least in this respect, races are like witches: however unreal witches are, *belief* in witches, like belief in races, has had—and in many communities continues to have—profound consequences for human social life. (p. 277)

So even though we may intellectually dismiss race as an essentialized concept, we still must take it into account when looking at social settings and interactions, as race still very much is a crucial and material social construct in everyday existence.

The assumption is, then, that when people speak of race, they are talking about some way in which the world of humans has been divided. The most apparent of the markers by which these divisions has been made is physical appearance. Black, brown, red, yellow, and white skin is one system of classification. African, Latino, Native American, Asian, Caucasian might be another set of terms used to carve people up into similar categories, but it still comes down to skin color, which has become one of the most powerful ways in which people distinguish between one another, as was pointed out by François Raveau (1968):

> But what could be more striking than the color of the skin? All other distinctions fade before this basic one. A black, yellow, or white man immediately stands out in an environment where people have skins of different color. This definitive barrier cannot be bridged by any artifice. (pp. 98–99)

In addition to skin color, there are body shapes and sizes, hair color and texture, facial characteristics, like the shape of one's eyes or the size of one's nose. Other features people use to delineate include hair styles, clothing, jewelry, articulated beliefs, language, or accent. Each of these is a symbol, which people use as they try to construct a person's identity. The assigning of a person to a racial group, then, is a historically situated, symbolic, socially constructed process, ultimately decentered and one that changes not only from locale to locale, but even within locales depending on circumstances and contexts. Racial classification is anything but static (Lieberson & Waters, 1988). This process is influenced by a number of factors, including an individual's socialization, class status, and of course by commonly accepted beliefs that are often strongly influenced by political factors. Omi and Winant (1986) argued effectively that the determining of race and racial groups is a highly politicized process.

Ethnicity is a term taken from the Greek ethnikos, which refers to the people from a particular nation. But just as scholars have not been able to contain humans in biological racial classifications, national boundaries have provided an equally ineffective method of defining or categorizing people. Problems here lie in the fact that people from the same nation may not be at all alike whether in cultural practices or in language or skin color. Even with more defined groups within nations, for example, subgroups identified by color, there may still be tremendous diversity. For example, within the United States, we can hardly link together meaningfully Japanese-, Korean-, Vietnamese-, Laotian-, Chinese-, Cambodian- (etc.) Americans as Asian-Americans. And there are even further distinctions within these subgroups, say, between Okinawins and other Japanese-Americans.

It is extremely problematic to set limits to or put boundaries around identity. Barth (1969) pointed out that ethnic boundaries should not be uncritically accepted as fixed. Barth contended that ethnic boundaries, like racial boundaries, are socially created. What this means ultimately is that ethnicity is also an inexact term. What Barth and others have helped us understand is that one's ethnicity is a remarkably complex matter, influenced by different factors, including skin color, national or community heritage, religious belief, language, class status, and social orientation. As with race, the concept of ethnicity, although complex and unstable, is widely held by people as something very transparent, something easily identified.

One difference between the terms ethnicity and race is that in this century we have come to identify closely the term ethnicity with the idea of distinctions between groups within one skin color. For instance, Park (1914), Glazer and Moynahan (1963), and others wrote about ethnic distinctions between groups of European immigrants to America. Thus, ethnicity became more closely identified with distinctions between the Irish and the Germans, or the French and the Polish. Yet again, to separate race out as a distinct category does not work here, because within these national groups, there are people with many different colors of skin. No sooner has one offered a definition of ethnicity, then it can be effectively challenged. Thus, ethnicity, like race, is a term often used without considering the full implications of the concept.

That one might see the terms race and ethnicity used either side by side, or even at times interchangeably, can be attributed to overlap and slippage between distinctions that in both cases are social constructions. Thus, the sometimes contradictory or contentious discourse of race and ethnicity might be compared to the discourse of sex and gender, also long thought to be essentialized "natural" categories that have in more recent times been problematized into a more complex dialogue about the very categories of male and female.

In regard to the terminology used to talk about race and/or ethnicity, some authors have chosen to use a hyphenated version, such as race-ethnicity (Ringer & Lawless, 1989). In what follows, both terms are used by informants, but when I refer to the symbolic, socially created system that people use to try to determine others' identity, the term used is race-ethnicity. When referring to people who have been racially marked or identified as different than the norm of American White by physical or cultural characteristics, the term used is people of color.

## ANALYTICAL FRAMEWORKS

What follows is the general theoretical framework used as a starting point for this research project. There are two primary ideas that set the stage for what is ahead. The goal is to take these paradigms or these theoretical positions and use them to help understand what is going on in the two newsrooms in the two communities involved in the study.

The first theoretical framework for analysis appropriate to the questions that need to be asked about news coverage of people of color is hegemonic theory. Hegemony might be described as the process by which one group maintains power in a culture by maintaining the consensus of other groups.

Although certainly not unique to communication as a discipline, a number of communication theorists have worked in this area to gain a better understanding of how power works in and through mass media. Martín-Barbero (1987), building on the work of Williams and Hoggart, spoke generally about culture as the sphere of action of hegemony, and more specifically about media as a site where one might examine this process. Specifically Martín-Barbero discussed "those transformations of social legitimation which lead away from imposition of submission toward the search for consensus" (p. 85). Hall (1977) focused on how the dominant class "sets the limits—mental and structural—within which subordinate classes 'live' and make sense of their subordination in such a way as to sustain the dominance of those ruling over them" (p. 333). Lull (1995) said,

Owners and managers of media industries can produce and repro-
duce the content, inflections, and tones of ideas favorable to them
far more easily than other social groups because they manage key so-
cializing institutions, thereby guaranteeing their points of view are
consistently and attractively cast into the public arena. (p. 33)

Tuchman (1978a) wrote about how specifically the news media de-
termines the frames through which we as a culture view events, and
that the frames that are created ultimately sustain the status quo.
Gitlin (1980) explained in more detail how the framing process
takes place, often without the acknowledgment of the news workers
involved:

Normally the dominant frames are taken for granted by media practitioners, and reproduced and defended by them for reasons, and via
practices, which the practitioners do not conceive to be hegemonic.
Hegemony operates effectively—it does deliver the news—yet outside consciousness; it is exercised by self-conceived professionals
working with a great deal of autonomy within institutions that pro-
claim the neutral goal of informing the public. (pp. 257–258)

When it comes to analyzing two particular news organizations,
we must look critically at the way in which news decisions are made,
how story ideas are selected, and how news is gathered and pro-
duced to try to determine whether news workers in these specific locales are attempting to incorporate marginal and radical voices, or,
whether, as hegemonic theory would suggest, they are simply repro-
ducing and reifying ideas that sustain the power structure, both culturally and economically. Interviews with marginalized community
members can shed some critical light on whether people perceive
that a news organization is representing disenfranchised voices, or
whether indeed journalistic practice continues to primarily support
the ideas and the agenda of those in power in the culture.

Because this study is concerned with local news organizations'
treatment specifically of people of color, the other pertinent para-
digm involves the social construction of race, and how certain media practices may constitute a form of racism. For this analysis the
framework established by Essed (1991) may prove most helpful.

Essed effectively pulled together a number of different aspects of behavior, both personal and social, into a framework of what she called everyday racism. She argued, as have others (e.g., Omi & Winant, 1986), that racism is not a permanent feature of a society, but instead is reproduced out of a complex set of conditions. Her framework may provide a helpful starting point by which one could analyze daily activities in a local newsroom. Although a comprehensive breakdown of all the social interactions, spoken and unspoken, that occur within even one newsroom would be a monumental if even achievable task, a more modest goal may be to use Essed's framework to glean some information about news workers' perceptions about race-ethnicity and how that may influence the daily process of news gathering: "[A] major feature of everyday racism is that it involves racist practices that infiltrate everyday life and become part of what is seen as 'normal' by the dominant group" (p. 288). Essed's idea is that racism should no longer be compartmentalized into structural or personal categories, but instead, researchers should focus on the ways in which these categories are linked:

> The concept of "everyday" was introduced to cross boundaries between structural and interactional approaches to racism and to link the details of micro experiences to the structural and ideological context in which they are shaped. The analysis of these experiences has shown that everyday racism does not exist as single events but as a complex of cumulative practices. (p. 288)

In the context of news production, that means researchers need to strive to understand how something like the ownership of television stations and the day-to-day practice of news production may work together to systematically exclude certain groups of people, or how large-scale economic discrimination and small-scale daily coverage decisions are also ultimately contributing to similar ends: continued marginalization of people of color.

The paradigms of hegemony and everyday racism may provide not only the theoretical background needed for analysis, but also some of the analytical tools by which some sense may be made out of the data gathered in the field.

What follows is a detailed discussion, description, and analysis of what I found during my time in Honolulu and Albuquerque. The discussion begins with a look at how newsrooms work, how news decisions are made, and by whom. Thus, chapter 1 is primarily about news decision-making power. Chapter 2 is an analysis of news coverage of communities of color, with a detailed discussion of what stories are most often covered and what stories are often left with little or no coverage. Chapter 2 also introduces the idea of *incognizant racism*, the primary theoretical contribution of this book. Chapter 3 deals with issues of whether citizens have access to newsrooms and news coverage. Geography's role on coverage is discussed in chapter 4. In chapter 5, I look at how a lack of historical context influences coverage and coverage decisions. Chapter 6 is the book's conclusion, and chapter 7 reviews some possible remedies to the issues raised here.

# Chapter 1

## News Power

As the means of information and of power are centralized, some men will come to occupy positions in American society from which they can look down upon, so to speak, and by their decisions mightily affect, the everyday worlds of ordinary men and women.

—C. Wright Mills

Journalists enjoy autonomy, yet that freedom takes place within the constraints of an organizational culture and structure. To understand how and why certain content does or does not end up on the air in a particular local station's newscasts, it is important to understand the process and structure that govern news decision making. This includes considering questions of ownership. Having spent some time working in and observing newsrooms, it is apparent there are few overt dictums or conspiracies when it comes to deciding what will or will not become part of a nightly newscast. So it will be in processes that are naturalized that one might find clues as to whether hegemony and everyday racism take place, and if so exactly how these theoretical positions are fleshed out in the routines of news workers.

## NEWS PROCESS

In most local television newsrooms, the news process begins in the morning. Assignment editors arrive and begin setting the news agenda for the day. At some operations, the day's activities are planned out the night before. It is all part of the news process, wherein a set of actions is set into motion that results in an afternoon and evening newscast. Those newscasts are filled with stories, some about the events of the day, with a wide range of topics from health to politics to the weather. From other research, we know that seemingly few of those stories will concern people of color. If they do, that coverage will often be about crime. But what seems to be lacking is substantive coverage about issues that may most affect communities of color. To understand why, one must understand this news process, and who controls the process.

Most local news operations have a news agenda for each day. The items for that agenda are gathered from a number of different sources and are usually compiled by an assignment editor. The assignment editor is a mid-level manager in a newsroom whose responsibilities generally include setting the day's agenda first thing in the morning, then monitoring where news crews are through radio and pager contact, sorting through information sent, faxed, and phoned into the newsroom during the day, and checking with other news managers to see what their wishes are in terms of the needs and wants for the afternoon and evening newscasts. The assignment editor is the person who generally keeps up on all that is going on during the day, tries to make sure news crews get to the right place at the right time, and attempts to see that no breaking news stories are missed.

Stories in the two newsrooms in this study, as they would in many newsrooms, came from a variety of different sources. Newspapers and other broadcast news operations were closely monitored and often served as sources for stories. News workers also monitored the wire service for story ideas. News releases and announcements of news conferences provided another potential source of news stories. Reporters often turned in story ideas, and other news workers such as photographers and producers also on occasion turned in story ideas. There were also police and fire scanners present, so that news workers would know if there was any kind of emergency or breaking news. In both newsrooms studied, all of these sources were used to generate ideas that were then compiled into a list that was reviewed at the beginning of the day.

In the newsroom in Albuquerque, a morning news meeting was held to discuss coverage decisions. Generally present at that meeting were the news director (but not always), the executive producer, the assignment editor, newscast producers, some reporters, some photographers, and at times, an anchor.

There was no morning news meeting in the Honolulu newsroom. Instead, the assignment editor reviewed potential stories, set a preliminary agenda for the day and went over that agenda with the news director for approval.

Both newsrooms had similar organizational structures. The Albuquerque newsroom was headed by a news director, who was the department head in charge of personnel, budget, and editorial decisions for the newsroom. Second in charge was the executive producer, who was in close contact with the news director, and was primarily responsible for the day-to-day management of the newsroom, especially in regard to editorial control of on-air content. In Honolulu, there was a news director who was in charge of the newsroom. Next there were three managers, a managing editor, an executive producer, and an assistant news director who took care of a variety of different responsibilities.

The next tier of management in both newsrooms fell on people in two different positions. First, assignment editors, whose responsibilities were already discussed, and next, producers, who are the workers who actually assemble and coordinate news programs. In these news operations, as with many others, one producer was assigned to each news show. There is a pecking order within the assignment editors that is usually delineated by shift. The senior-most person works week days, the next most senior week day evenings, and so on. With producers, the most senior producer is often assigned to the show perceived as the most critical to the station, often the 6 p.m. or 10 p.m. program.

In Albuquerque, there are three central 30-minute newscasts, all considered important to the news operation, that air respectively at 5 p.m., 6 p.m., and 10 p.m. All three producers seemed to share responsibilities, although the 10 p.m. producer had more editorial leeway, as most other managers had gone home by the time he was actually assembling his newscast. In Honolulu, the primary newscasts are an hour-long program at 5 p.m. and a 30-minute program at 10 p.m. Both producers have their programs supervised and approved by both the executive producer and the news director.

The explanation of these positions is offered because, in the news operations studied, it is these positions wherein most of the decision-making power lies when it comes to what will and will not be part of daily newscasts.

## NEWS MANAGERS

It was crucial to identify in each newsroom exactly where decision-making power was located. Interviews with news workers confirmed what I had seen in other newsrooms and what had been observed in these newsrooms. No matter the size of the operation, no matter the actual number of employees in the newsroom, decision-making power generally lies in the hands of just a few managers.

The most senior assignment editor in Albuquerque understood the control he had over coverage, which was due to the fact that he was the one who started the coverage process each weekday:

> The executive producer has a great deal of input on what's going on. But in coming in and starting the day I think I have a significant impact on what's seen on the news.

Assignment editors, due to the fact that they set the daily agenda and then often are most directly in contact with crews in the field, are afforded control. But they are not alone. Newscast producers also have varying amounts of control as to what will and will not go into their program. Ultimate authority, however, generally rests with the two or three people at the top of the news organizational chart. News directors and their assistants, either holding titles of executive producer, assistant news director, or managing editor, over-see the overall operation and have ultimate decision-making authority. That certainly held true in both Albuquerque and Hono-lulu. A reporter in Hawai'i noted:

> The way we are organized now, the managing editor has the most to say during the day. It may change following the managers' meeting in the afternoon, but day-to-day he has the most to say.

Although news coverage and content decisions are often dis-cussed as the day progresses, most newsrooms have regularly sched-uled news meetings. Often there are two meetings, one in the morning to get the day underway, and then one in the afternoon to bring night shift managers up to speed and to finalize plans for the early evening newscasts. At the two stations in this study, news meetings were held, but varied tremendously between stations. In Albuquerque there were two news meetings, one in the morning and one in the afternoon. The meeting was often run by the senior assignment editor. It was attended always by other assignment edi-tors, show producers, and the executive producer. Others including the news director, reporters, photographers, anchors, and other news workers, joined in on a less than regular basis. Some in the newsroom chose not to attend the meetings at all.

In Honolulu, there was no morning meeting. Instead, in the morning the assignment editor would, at times, go over the news agenda with the news director and they would select the stories for that day. At other times, the senior assignment editor (who had the title of managing editor) would select the stories without talking to the news director, depending on the news director's availability. In the afternoon, the managing editor, the executive producer and the 5 p.m. and 10 p.m. producers would meet with the news director in his office to discuss what would be aired on the station's nightly newscasts. The physical size of the office precluded anyone else par-ticipating in the meetings, unless they were called in by the manag-ers to give a brief update on a story. For instance, a reporter might be summoned to step into the doorway and bring the managers up to date on how his or her story was coming together. After some discussion, the reporter would leave and the discussion would continue. News workers knew this was where news decisions were made, but because they did not participate, they were not always sure who made those decisions. This was demonstrated by a reporter who had worked at the station for several years.

> Who has the most control over what gets on the air? That would have to be the managing editor, the executive producer and the news director. Its really hard to say which one because we don't sit in on these meetings.

In both newsrooms, reporters and others can suggest story ideas, and often, after approval from management, these stories do get on the air. But reporters and other news workers ultimately do not have the power to decide even what stories they will work on day to day.

Who are the managers who make these decisions? At both stations, top news managers were all White males. Wilson and Gutiérrez (1985, 1995) documented the fact that Whites have consistently remained the gatekeepers of U.S. media. Evidence of this contention is plentiful, ranging from reports from the U.S. Commission on Civil Rights (1977, 1979) to Stone's (1993) work. Stone conducted research for the Radio and Television News Directors' Association (RTNDA) for a number of years, and repeatedly documented the lack of women and people of color in broadcast newsrooms. Stone found that minorities make up 18.5% of the broadcast news workforce. Hispanics account for only 6% of the television news workforce. Stone found that minorities make up only 8.7% of television news directors. In an earlier survey, Stone (1988) discovered a disproportionate number of minority workers were holding positions as camera operators, one of the lowest paying jobs in TV news. He also found because of "dead ends" in broadcast news, minorities in general, and Blacks in particular, had been leaving broadcast news for better opportunities in other fields. In 1996, RTNDA released more current figures (Papper, Gerhard, & Sharma, 1996) indicating little change in management, with only 9% of news director positions filled by minorities. In decision-making positions, Whites still make up the majority of news directors (91%), assistant news directors (90%), executive producers (93%), managing editors (85%), assignment editors (84%), and producers (86%).

People of color have made very few inroads into television news management. So even in areas where people of color may make up a large portion or even the majority of the population, those who remain in control of news programming most often do not reflect the make-up of the population covered by the news organization.

According to critiques of news coverage from inside and outside of the two newsrooms, having White men at the top contributes to a lack of coverage of people of color. Gene Hill, a community activist and radio talk show host in Albuquerque, believes the race-ethnicity of news managers (i.e., White) has contributed negatively to coverage of people of color:

> Look at the structure of this station here or any station: top management—Anglo. A few brown faces at the anchor desk and stuff like that and secretaries and so on. So the policies are going to continue to be very racist.

This impression is echoed by a White, male producer in Albuquerque:

> I think most of the decision makers in this news room are white men. I think that any time you have that there's going to be a lack of, you know, any kind of insight into how to make decisions about how to cover stories that come up.

## PEOPLE OF COLOR
## AND DECISION MAKING

People of color did sit in on news meetings in both newsrooms, but they did not occupy positions of power, thus they did not have the opportunity to make final decisions about what events and issues would or would not be contained in the newscast.

This is not to say, however, that people of color did not participate, and many, at times, were able to add perspective to what decisions are made. In Honolulu, both the 5 p.m. and 10 p.m. newscast producers were Asian American. They sat in on the afternoon news meeting and they contributed daily to the news process. However, that news meeting, the primary forum where daily news content is discussed, took place well into the day, after most coverage decisions had already been made. In essence, the content of the two shows had been set into motion hours earlier and although some shifting was possible, wholesale changes by that time of the day are difficult, if not impossible.

In Albuquerque, the news meetings were held in a conference room large enough that anyone could participate, and often did. In this newsroom, one of the three nightly newscast producers was Hispanic, the other two were White. The newsroom also employed an African-American reporter, and an Asian-American reporter, and several other staffers who were people of color. The station's on-air presence was very integrated, especially in regard to Latinos. The morning anchor was Hispanic, the anchor team for the 5 p.m. news consisted of an Hispanic woman and a Native American man (one of the remarkably few Native Americans in TV news in the country), the 6 and 10 p.m. anchor team consisted of a Hispanic woman and a White man. Weather and sports anchors were all White men.

Although this diverse on-air presence was a relatively recent development, it was the source of pride for many people at the station. Yet, anchors most often are not considered people who should or do exercise influence on on-air content. Evening anchors often do not arrive at the station until 1 or 2 p.m., again, after the news agenda for the day is set. Often, the anchors who were present at the station when a news meeting occurred were otherwise occupied. One minority anchor put it this way:

> The fact is that everything comes through a couple of key individuals. It concerns me that if I'm not there or someone of color is not in those editorial meetings, the content of our newscasts gets covered by their perception.

There were times in Albuquerque editorial meetings where no people of color were present. There were also times where I observed people of color present and contributing vigorously to the discussion. But no matter the level of participation, the news decision-making power remained in the hands of White managers, a fact not lost on the people who work at the station, including one Hispanic anchor:

> There are a few of us who are lucky to have very good, high profile, high paying positions. We talk about how careful we want to be that that's never misconstrued to let people believe that there have been great strides because we're absent in management throughout the state.

Although it is difficult to discern the public perception of the station, several people outside the station who were interviewed were very much aware of the contradiction of having people of color on the air, yet not in key decision-making positions.

> There's a brown face up there saying it. So we're supposed to be very happy because they got brown faces over there as anchors? Well, the anchors don't matter. (Gene Hill)

> They've had anchors, a few here and there. But who decides the policy? Who decides the criteria and makes the decision for coverage? That's where it's all at. (Michael Guerrero)

## PEOPLE OF COLOR AS ANCHORS, NOT MANAGERS

It may not be a coincidence that people of color end up in anchor instead of management positions. The anchor jobs are highly visible positions, which make them important in terms of people's perceptions of the television stations. Anchor positions are often sought after by news workers because they offer an opportunity to make more money, at times significantly more money, than do other positions in the newsroom. There are also other benefits such as a decreased workload, clothing and make-up allowances, and a certain amount of prestige and recognition within the community. At some stations, there might be both the influence of managers who are intentionally trying to put more people of color into highly visible on-air positions, plus the broadcaster's own desire for a high-prestige, highly paid position. There are also agents and head-hunting firms that seek talented people of color and encourage them to take lucrative anchor positions. One long-time anchor has seen the phenomenon in her own career and wonders whether the decision by young journalists to select anchoring as a career is made without full consideration of how newsrooms operate.

> Most minorities that come out of J-School are sought after by agents or by these markets to be on air. And I think a lot of them are drawn to it. They see that's where the money potential is and to feed their ego. I don't think they're thinking about where the power is. I don't think they know much about how a news room runs.

Entman (1990, 1992), in his studies of Chicago television, discussed the idea that the very presence of African Americans in anchor positions "may engender an impression that racial discrimination is no longer a problem" (p. 342). Yet, his studies indicated components of what he called modern racism in day-to-day news coverage of the Black community. In the same way here, having people of color, Black or otherwise, in anchor positions may lead viewers to incorrect assumptions about the racial-ethnic make-up of a television station's staff, about the racial-ethnic make-up of station management, and again, ultimately about decisions made in regard to coverage of people of color. A producer in Albuquerque summed it up this way:

> They know that we will come off more politically correct if we have minorities on the air, if people of color are on the air then we don't look so much like a bunch of white boys telling you what's important in today's events. And that can be deceiving you know. I think you have to continually look at content and it really is controlled by a bunch of white boys. You wouldn't get that watching us on the air because the presenters are not white, but the people who are making the decisions are and I think that's an interesting notion, you know, the distinction between content and presentation.

The trend toward keeping people of color out of management positions does not seem to be changing with time. One reporter explained the continuity in the number of White managers this way:

> All you have to do is look at who's on top. You tend to choose people, I believe, like yourself. It's always going to match, to reproduce itself, because the old guys will pick the new guys. You're not going to get a diverse group.

There are other assumptions to be examined about the link between race-ethnicity of news managers and the decisions they make. For instance, does skin color necessarily determine cultural sensitivity? Simply being White or Black or Brown does not guarantee that you will be sensitive to issues crucial to communities of color. The inverse holds true as well. There may indeed be Anglo managers who might go out of their way to ensure broad-based and diverse coverage of many different groups of people. It would be difficult to argue that every Anglo manager makes news decisions in exactly the same fashion, Anglo or not. van Zoonen (1988), in regard to women and news, argued that simply increasing the number of women in management positions would not guarantee a qualitative change in the form or substance of the news. van Zoonen argued that when it comes to the construction of news, there are always complicating factors that must be considered. First, an individual's gender or skin color may not be the guiding influence on what decision he or she might make when it comes to making decisions about news coverage. There may be other factors such as individual values, class background, or professional norms that could also influence these kinds of decisions. As well, by assuming that women or people of color would produce different news coverage infers that individuals are given leeway to make independent decisions.

> Research on news production has shown that the individual journalist works in the midst of social, organizational and ideological factors that jointly shape news content. The autonomy of individual journalists must, at least, be questioned. (van Zoonen, 1988, p. 45)

This raises the question of organizational norms and expectations. The construction of news is based on principles that have been carried out year after year. People who are new in the organization are expected to learn these norms and continue carrying on the traditions. News practice is something professionals spend very little time examining and reformulating. Accepted conventions and routines are difficult to break from, having been taught in college and high school journalism programs and reinforced throughout news workers' careers. Most news professionals grew up watching and reading news, gaining some sense from an early age what news is and is not, or more accurately what has been traditionally accepted as what does and does not constitute events that would be considered acceptable for presentation on a news program.

Simple changes in the racial-ethnic make-up of news managers may not guarantee changes in these long-held traditions. Soloski (1989) examined how professional norms may influence news content. He argued that one of these norms is for reporters primarily to rely on sources within the existing power structure, therefore very little outside of the mainstream gets reported.

> Although journalists do not set out to report the news so that the existing politco-economic system is maintained, their professional norms end up producing stories that implicitly support the existing order. In addition, the professional norms legitimize the existing order by making it appear to be the natural state of affairs. The tenets of news professionalism result in news coverage that does not threaten either the economic position of the individual news organization or the overall politico-economic system in which the news organization operates. (Soloski, 1989, p. 225)

It is not enough to simply argue that adding more people of color to management ranks will necessarily generate changes in coverage of communities of color. Other factors may be as (or more) critical. For instance, what is the economic or social class background of managers? For the mayor of Santa Fe, class and race are issues that go hand in hand when it comes to determining how a news manager may decide what is and what is not newsworthy.

That person at the very top, who gives the directives, is not some-one, and has never been, in my mind, someone who is a people per-son, who is a minority, who is someone who can understand what a social ill is and what we can do to solve them. They are in a business to make money and so they operate like businesses. I've never be-lieved that the media is out there to really have people be informed about their environment. What do you think they are there for? To stay in power. To make sure they are able to continue to do what they like to do and be who they are, and hold on to that power and don't give it to anyone, once they've got it, who's going to give it away or let go of it. (Debbie Jaramillo)

## OWNERSHIP, LOCALISM, AND NEWS PHILOSOPHY

When talking about news coverage, it also is crucial to consider cor-porate ownership and corporate policy. For instance, even if there were to be significant influx in the number of people of color in the news management ranks, there is no guarantee any changes would occur in the make-up of who owns the media outlets. A traditional view of commercial television posited that the viewers were the consumers, and were allowed to watch programs paid for by spon-sorship by commercial interests. However, in his critique of Cana-dian broadcasting, Smythe (1981) made a strong case that it is viewers' attention that is being sold to commercial interests. In other words, viewers' attention is the product, being sold to compa-nies that buy that attention from television stations. This commodi-fication of the audience may explain much when it comes to understanding why television stations make certain decisions. Since the 1970s, television news increasingly has become a profit center for local television news operations. This has had an impact on not only the commercial content of television, but on programs as well, including news programs. Altschull (1984) wrote exten-sively about how local news reflects the ideology of the station own-ers. It is not that local newscasts will contain blatant messages, but instead that in general, coverage reflects support of capitalism. Altschull also said that in general audiences are given more soft news and less information about politics or economics or other areas that could be socially significant. That would mean that when stations air newscasts, the motive would generally not be to give viewers information that might be critical of the status quo, but instead, these newscasts would simply be filled with superficial reporting. If Smythe's argument holds, the aim of these newscasts would be to help a station make more money, not necessarily to provide the audience with more information. Entman (1989) argued that the competition for viewers prevents television journalists from "supplying the kind of news that would allow the average citizen to practice sophisticated citizenship" (p. 17). McManus (1989) discovered that there was some support for his hypothesis that economic considerations may be more important than professional considerations when it comes to news coverage. In a study of three stations in three different markets, McManus found stations were putting more low-assembly cost stories on the air than high assembly cost stories. Busterna (1980, 1988) discovered that competition and market size were positively related to local television news expenditures. Altheide and Rasmussen (1976) spent extensive time studying two network affiliates and concluded that the stations were "more concerned with capturing the largest share of the audience through entertaining news items than grappling with the complexities of issues and problems." Bagdikian (1983) argued that America's capitalist system has had an impact on news media, forcing news operations to present a homogenized version of the news, diluted of any real meaning and "filled with frivolous material" (p. 206). Postman (1985) also has written that television news is more concerned with amusement than providing important information. So, it seems, television news is an institution where there may be little opportunity or motivation for in-depth coverage of serious issues.

Currently, ample evidence exists that most broadcast outlets are owned by White-dominated corporations. Often, local stations are owned by large chains, more often than not, with corporate headquarters in locations far from the local news operation. Not only do the stations have long-distance owners, but there is rarely consideration given to the geographic background of the managers who run the station, and that includes news directors. An anchor in Hawai'i noted the following:

A lot of the TV stations news directors are not and have not been local people. I'm not saying they all should be or need only be, but they
usually come from out of state. And they come in with a really different perspective about what they think of what news people locally
should be seeing.

The news director in Honolulu was from Iowa. The news director in Albuquerque was from Minnesota. Both, although
open-minded, bring with them years of life experience growing up in
the midwest, not in Hawai'i or New Mexico, both of which are
places very different in history and culture than Minnesota or Iowa.
The news director in Honolulu was not convinced that where he
came from was negatively impacting his ability to makes news decisions in Hawai'i.

Is news different in Hawai'i than it is Iowa? I'm not a bit convinced
that it is. I'm not a bit convinced of that. No, I don't see any reason
that it should be. I mean, I think that what you're doing in news is
covering the interests of people, and I think that those items of interest are going to be pretty much the same. I think news is pretty much
news.

What this news director reveals is a belief that news events happen,
and reporters simply record, organize, and broadcast those events to
the public, no matter the locale. This assumption does not take into
account the many layered process of decision making that takes
place before any story is chosen for the news. There is no consideration of the very process of how information gets into the news
room, how that information is filtered by news managers, and then
what goes into the decision-making process becomes naturalized.
Why is it that that each night only certain events somehow rise to
the top of the news agenda? Is it because they are the most important and pertinent to the community, or is it because news workers,
due to homogeneity of backgrounds and socialization of news
norms, repeatedly select the same stories? Carey (1989) argued for a
model of news as ritual, wherein the news-gathering and dissemination process provides little truly new knowledge, but instead serves

to reify, or reenact and reinforce the already existing views of the world.

What is not overt in the news director's comments are an underlying assumption that what is interesting and pertinent to one person will indeed be interesting and pertinent to any other person, no matter locale, cultural background, race-ethnicity, or class standing. That some news items may have universal appeal is not the question here, instead this study questions whether the news product as an entirety is truly reflective and inclusive of a number of diverse ideas and viewpoints. This is part of the process Essed (1991) discusses in *Understanding Everyday Racism*. Essed pointed out that there is among Whites a naturalized belief that all people think the same way, that all people given similar circumstances would make the same decisions, or that all people, in this case, would select the same news stories. These kinds of assumptions are made by Whites who have never fully experienced life from a different, nonmainstream perspective.

> Hidden under the surface of diversity, there is a strong tendency among Whites, in the United States as well as in the Netherlands, to assume the superiority of Euro-American values. Hidden also is the expectation that, in due time, Blacks must accept that the norms and values of the Euro-American tradition are superior and that adaptation is the only way to progress is society. (p. 189)

The Honolulu news director assumes his newscast has such diversity, because his program dominates local ratings.

> If we cover the community, well, then we are covering the ethnic groups in the community. If we don't, then we're not. Now how do we know if we are or we're not? Well, there's lots of ways teachers would like to think about that or researchers, but I think there's only one way. If the community accepts what you're doing and welcomes you into their home then you're probably doing it very well. Because they're going to do it otherwise, they're going to go somewhere else.

The question that remains is whether any stations in the market offer news from a diverse perspective, and if not, where else could viewers turn?

The news director in New Mexico talked about the news coverage process in slightly different terms. He talked about executing his
news philosophy by trying to find stories that would have broad audience appeal, and he talked about his viewers as his customers.

> It's news for our viewers, and that is the most important thing—the
> viewers. It's news if it affects people and or interests people. That's as
> basic as it gets. That's what makes a story. That is if it interests people
> widely or affect them broadly that's the stories we'll do.

This is a news philosophy where ratings become the ultimate gauge of
what viewers want. The idea is that if a station is providing viewers with
what they want, then they will watch, if not, they won't watch. What
this does not take into account are the many other reasons people may
choose to view a particular news product, such as the personality of anchors. The programs preceding the local news program may also have a
great influence on which news program viewers may watch. And as discussed earlier, it is not as if there was a remarkably diverse selection of
local news programs from which to select. If stations are generally providing similar news programming, the decision to pick one station may
indeed have more to do with the appeal of anchor people or programming lead-ins than news content.

Even if trying to appeal to a large audience has a pluralistic sound
to it, it still comes down to a news philosophy that is based on a principal where the majority rules. In other words, if the majority of
viewers pick one station to watch, then it follows that the station's
coverage must be the most broad-based. But what does this mean
when it comes to covering stories that might not have obvious appeal to large segments of the audience? One person of color at the
Albuquerque station reported that because of this news standard,
news from alternative communities was difficult to sell to managers.

> I would say there's some difficulty getting a story on the air because I
> would say that those who sort out what gets on the air and what
> doesn't look at it with a lens that automatically set standards
> whether or not it affects a lot of people or whether or not it will inter-
> est a lot of people. Sort of the more broader appeal for a much
> broader audience, and if it doesn't have those kind of requisites, I
> don't think it gets on the air.

In other words, if a story does not appeal to a majority of the audience, which in New Mexico could mean the majority White audience, then it may not pass muster. In Albuquerque, even though there is some argument over whether Whites still hold the majority in terms of population, the television stations, through market research, are still acutely aware of who makes up their audience. As for the station in this study, the sales department indicated the station was watched by people with an attractive demographic profile (i.e., people with spending power). This means the station is still very much trying to appeal to a White audience. There is also an underlying assumption that people of color do not have spending power, despite a considerable Hispanic middle and upper class. The bottom line remains that the station is still acutely aware of its White viewers, and principals of majority rules still apply. As Essed (1991) pointed out, this decision-making principal is often lorded over people who are not in the majority:

> Dominant values, conceptions of reality, and style habits are further reinforced through majority rule. There is reason to believe that what Marcuse has called the "tyranny of the majority" has specific repercussions for race relations. Majority rule can may be experienced as "tyranny" when the oppression of Black women is repeatedly legitimized through majority decisions in everyday decisions. This is the problem when the dominant group does not problemitize racism in society. (p. 204)

Or when those dominant values are reinforced by news values that do not allow space for alternative perspectives. In the newsrooms studied, as is true in almost all television newsrooms in the country, majority rules still means rule by the White majority. In Albuquerque, it meant the people who were making the decisions about what is or is not appealing to the audience were White managers, who in this case were not from New Mexico.[1]

---

[1] In Albuquerque and Honolulu, both news directors reported consultants had little influence over their news decision making. This study was not particularly designed to look at the news consultants' influence on local news, and no news workers mentioned consultants influence in their interviews, however, it may be another factor in why there is homogeneity between different stations in different locales.

Would hiring local people guarantee different coverage? Perhaps not, but it would put people in decision-making positions who do not have to unlearn years of education, socialization, and cultural orientation to begin understanding a sense of place and localism.

Both stations in this study had histories of hiring news managers who were neither local, nor people of color. An assistant news director in Hawai'i summed up that fact as follows:

> I think its because the media outlets here are owned by mainland companies, white mainland companies, and they sent their people out here and the people that they are sending out are generally like the people who own the places.

Again, there is no guarantee that if a station is locally owned, coverage might look significantly different. But the fact that station owners are thousands of miles away means simply that they do not live in or experience daily life in Hawai'i or New Mexico. And the owners do not see daily examples of the news product their own organization is putting on the air. Therefore, those in ultimate control of these news-gathering organizations are far removed from the very people and community that their news product may affect.

Ownership, professional norms, social, economic, and racial-ethnic backgrounds of managers all figure in to some explanation of why news coverage may look like it does. The fact remains, we still do not know what local TV news might look like with people of color, or local people, or people from varied class backgrounds in control, because this is a scenario that remains extremely far-fetched, given the industry's consistent practice of hiring and promoting primarily White men into management positions. At this time, we are left to continue examining current news practice and to put on hold any hope of significant changes in terms of shifts in news conventions or even the racial-ethnic make-up of those who make the decisions regarding those conventions.

# Chapter 2
## News Coverage

*Injustice anywhere is a threat to justice everywhere. We are caught in an inescapable network of mutuality, tied in a single garment of destiny. Whatever affects one directly, affects all indirectly.*

—Martin Luther King, Jr.

Given that few people of color are in news management, and television station ownership historically has not been aggressively working to change that, it may be helpful to gain an understanding of how that may or may not impact local news coverage. As noted earlier, research has indicated a lack of coverage of people of color. This study gave people of color in two communities an opportunity to critique coverage.

There was an almost uniform consensus among people interviewed in the two communities for this research that coverage was lacking, and lacking to the point of being negligent. In regard to local TV news coverage of Latinos in Albuquerque, "on a 1 to 10 scale, probably a 3," said one source, who is the spokesperson for the police department and a Chicana community organizer. A syndicated newspaper columnist in Albuquerque said of local TV coverage, "It would be hard to give them an 'A' in any field except in covering the negative aspects of news as it touches the Hispanic community." A Samoan social worker in Hawai'i felt there were many things that were being missed in his community by local news coverage:

> Of course there is news out there to report. I think we deserve some spot, some time on TV and in the newspaper. And talk positively about us rather than presenting a negative image constantly. Every time something comes up in the paper relative to our people, I would say 90% of the time, it is bad. So if its not bad, its not news? And if its good, that's no news? That's our perception of the system in terms of news reporting.

Some people within the news operations also acknowledged a lack of coverage of people of color. The managing editor at the Honolulu station expressed fear at covering issues that might uncover deeper racial tension in the community.

> I think we could do a lot better job. I mean some of the stories are almost … things that are simmering that you know … it's like, sometimes I don't want to go out and do a story about this guy who beat up another guy because of their race. Because if it's true, maybe that's the case, but to speculate on that may make somebody, it's like doing a suicide story. "Let's do a story on teen suicide" well I don't know because how many kids may watch that think that's romantic and go out and kill themselves. I think in Hawai'i we don't do a lot of stories on ethnic tension.

A reporter in Albuquerque was also troubled by his station's coverage:

> In the TV business in general I'm not sure how to attack that, you've got to do today's news now with a limited number of people and it's kind of hard to delve into the deeper social issues when they're not on the front burner, but just bubbling away on the back. The older I get the more I worry about this stuff. I used to be a tough guy when I started, come on give me some police news, give some politician's news conference, and fire and some kind of minor bureaucratic scandal involving the taxpayers' money and there's a good mix for news, I don't know, I think we are leaving some stuff out. There's a lot more that goes on, particularly in this state, there's some very

complex traditional communities, groups of people who we just don't hear about on the news too much. We've got people living ways of life that are so different from what people experience in the vast suburbs of America out there and we don't often bring those stories home to our little suburbs and we don't always give a true picture of what the state is about.

Although these general critiques provide helpful anecdotal evidence that coverage of communities of color may be inadequate, it is crucial to delve deeper into the problem to understand exactly why that coverage is inadequate.

## COVERAGE PATTERNS

When speaking with informants inside the local news organizations or sources in local communities, a consensus also emerged as to the location of most coverage of people of color. The two topic areas identified were festivals and crime. The fact that two distinct categories were identified by so many people of color is in itself telling, given that communities of color and the people living in those communities are involved in every aspect of life, well beyond any artificial categories such as racial-ethnic festivals and crime. Analyzing both areas may reveal more about the way in which two local news operations make decisions about coverage of people of color in these two locales.

### Coverage of Festivals

Most of those interviewed indicated that coverage of people of color both in Albuquerque and in Honolulu most often centers around racial-ethnic festivals and celebrations.

Kevin Gover is a Native American attorney who represented several tribal governments in New Mexico. He now serves as Assistant Secretary–Indian Affairs for the U.S. Department of the Interior. Gover indicated that most coverage he saw did not center around issues:

> In the hard news it's poor, some of the, what would I call it? I call them soft pieces about things like in the trends section, or coverage of cultural events, is pretty good.

Those sentiments were echoed by many, including Jim Anthony, a native of Fiji who now resides on Oahu and leads an environmental group. He characterized news coverage as being centered primarily around:

> what I call the antiseptic things in life. You know, there's a Hula going on someplace. Hula's safe. Let's report Hula. Um, there's an ethnic festival going on down the road. Let's report that. That's safe. So then, there's a great margin of safety within which reportage takes place. But on things that are outside of that margin of safety, no. And the lines seem to be fairly clearly drawn. I think there are pictures in the heads of people who make decisions as to what's safe and what's not.

A Native American television journalist in Albuquerque was realistic about his colleagues' knowledge and understanding of issues that concern the New Mexico Pueblos. He almost always is asked to cover any issues concerning Native Americans. Although he does so willingly, he also wishes his colleagues took a more active role in getting to know more about the Pueblos and the people who populate them.

> I don't know many people in the newsroom that have ever been to a reservation, let alone a Pueblo. Unfortunately the only time we have exposure to Pueblos is when there is something that is pretty much staged and you go out there and cover the event, an arts and crafts show and that's the only time you see anything on TV, if there's an arts and crafts show, especially in New Mexico, or if there's a pow-wow of some kind, a real colorful event. But when it comes to stories that are out there, human interest or whatever, it's a whole different world, mind set, etcetera. A lot of it's cultural. I don't know if people here have taken time out to really understand that.

Although there was a consensus of opinion among the people of color inside and outside the TV stations in this study, that consensus was not shared by some of the White news workers. One veteran reporter in Hawai'i rated her station's coverage of racial-ethnic communities as very good:

> I think it's excellent. I don't think we deal with most groups as ethnic groups, but when we do, when there's something specific ethnically we cover it. Whether it be a Portuguese malasada festival, obon dance or whatever, I think we always include that. We don't exclude it because it's Japanese or because it's Portuguese or because it's a small minority or whatever.

It seems that when this reporter thinks of coverage, she immediately thinks about coverage of racial-ethnic festivals as the positive way in which her station is working to cover people of color in the community. None of the people of color interviewed suggested that stations should not, on occasion, cover a racial-ethnic festival or celebration. Coverage of such stories may indeed provide the public images of people demonstrating pride in cultural traditions. But if a station's coverage of a certain group is disproportionately of such festivals with little other coverage, such images may also serve to reinforce stereotypes of groups as being regressive. For instance, to see on television only pictures of Native Americans in costumes performing ancient rituals, may lead viewers to only view Native Americans as people who are locked in one historically situated era, that of the past. When such images are not also balanced with images and stories about Native Americans as business people, lawyers, doctors, computer software designers, and so on, this could well reinforce stereotypes already seen in an entire genre of motion pictures based on misconceptions of the historic west. Repeated images of Native Americans engaged in only one activity, whether dancing, making pottery, or selling jewelry, reduces a diverse and wide-ranging group of people into an oversimplified symbol for what they actually are.

This type of stereotyping is addressed by a number of authors. Wilson and Gutiérrez (1995) wrote the following:

> The technique developed by the mass media in dealing with racial minorities and others outside the mainstream involved symbols and stereotypes. The mass media, because they dealt with a wide audience, came to rely on symbols and stereotypes as shorthand ways of communicating through headlines, characters, and pictures. (p. 43)

Dates and Barlow (1990) described stereotypes as images that are socially constructed, "selective, partial, one dimensional, and distorted," and they wrote that such images are "frozen, incapable of growth, change innovation, or transformation" (p. 30). In relation to hegemonic theory, stereotyping offers an insight into the important struggle over issues of meaning and identity. Stereotypes offer those in power an opportunity to control the images, the very ideas by which entire groups of people are defined. If every time one hears "Hispanic" on local newscasts and then is shown images of mariachis or piñatas, it contributes to what the individual may think about that group of people, or as Lippman and others have put it, it contributes to the pictures in one's head. Think for a moment of Hawai'i. Is the picture that comes to mind of Hula? These pictures are not multidimensional. They do not offer room for nuance or diversity. They are in no way reflective of large, complex groups of people who generally defy classification.

Yet hegemony does not operate as a completely dominating and overpowering system in terms of simply excluding all thoughts, ideas, or both that might be contrary to a dominant viewpoint. Instead, hegemony often takes perspectives and incorporates them into the mainstream, often robbing them of their critical perspective. In this case, if newscasters are inclusive of Hispanics, or Native American, or Native Hawaiians in the form of stories about ethnic festivals, the illusion is they are covering that community. But in reality, although the local news in Hawai'i or New Mexico is including these groups occasionally in their coverage, the news item frequently is only included as long as it falls within a strictly regulated range of activities (i.e., playing music, dancing, dressing in traditional costumes). By airing primarily these kinds of stories, news decision makers are limiting the public's ability to see people of color in a wider range of roles.

Often, within these festivals, care is taken to introduce participants to the audience and to provide biographical details such as educational background, careers, and so on, but such details may not be included in news stories. So, whereas a cultural event may be a celebration of both the group's tradition and the individual accomplishments of members of a racial-ethnic group, this detail may be lost when condensed into a news story.

As well, there is nothing de facto threatening about these activities. There is nothing revolutionary or extreme generally about cultural festivals. They represent a set of traditional, normalized behaviors that are easily classified into existing belief systems. These activities say nothing about social injustice, about institutionalized discrimination, about economics or employment. Therefore, by continually airing primarily this type of story, newscasters participate in the hegemonic subversion of group identity, whether it be of Hispanics, Native Americans, or Native Hawaiians, or for that matter, any other marginalized group.

An Anglo anchor in Honolulu characterized his station's coverage of people of color in terms of racial-ethnic events:

> I mean, I know we do stories sometimes maybe about a Buddhist temple, you know the construction permits or something. Or a Japanese lantern ceremony down the Ala Wai Canal. Different news items happen from time to time. But I mean to my knowledge we don't make a conscious effort to say we've got each group on so many times a week or a month or ... we just kind of cover the news as it happens or it seems to be newsworthy.

The first assumption here is that coverage of people of color could be boiled down to some type of quota, such as deciding each day to cover one story about Native Hawaiians, and two stories about Japanese-Americans, and so on. Yet, in covering the more dominant culture, news workers never ask how many White stories should be done today. Such analysis oversimplifies the bigger issue, which is, how a news organization could cover the larger diverse community, ensuring that all news events were covered in a more inclusive way and that if reporters were truly in touch with a broad range of people from many racial-ethnic groups, stories about these communities would arise in a natural, more frequent manner, such as they do currently in regard to the dominant White culture.

This television anchor also tried to imply that there is little, if any, intentionality in decisions that are made as to what stories are or are not covered by the news organization each day. His view is that events simply happen, and the people at the TV stations cover them, instead of looking beneath the surface at the myriad of decisions that go into a decision as to whether a news organization will or will not cover an event. The complexity of these decisions becomes more apparent when one realizes that there are a number of issues and events each day to choose from, and there is no automatic set of events that presents itself day by day, although the news decision-making process has become so naturalized within newsrooms that to some workers it may seem so, just as it seems natural to cover people of color primarily when they are holding some kind of cultural event. One of the news managers at the Honolulu station said: "What we do are the easy stories: the folk dancing festivals, the cultural festivals, seldom do we pick beneath the surface of songs, dances, art shows, and cultural demonstrations."

## Coverage of Crime

People in the communities in this study also reported that other than racial-ethnic festivals, the other primary time people of color were seen on the news was in crime reporting. Ray Armenta has been active in the Chicano community in Albuquerque and has worked for the Equal Employment Opportunity Commission:

> I feel candidly, I'll tell you, I feel like too much is focused on the negative. We get a lot of publicity that's usually on all the crime we have or say we have a Hispanic villain and the focus is on all the bad he did, instead on anything positive in the community, you know? I think it's just ingrained in the system that hasn't really accepted the fact that people of color are also educated and do good.

The assignment editor in Albuquerque defended his station's coverage of crime:

> Excessive coverage of people of color and crime? I don't think there is. When something comes over the scanner they don't say its a black, male shooting another black male, or three Hispanics gunned down a white woman or something like that, it's just a scene. And we

go by that scene and we cover the scene and if the scene is an important scene, it makes air. I don't think we try to focus on any one particular group. The scanner is color blind.

But people inside and outside TV news in Albuquerque tended to support the idea that there was disproportionate and a different type of coverage for crime in Albuquerque, depending on the color of skin of perpetrators or victims, and the geographic location of the crime itself. Activist and talk show host Gene Hill was most direct in his assessment:

> They sensationalize all the crime and there's plenty of it to sensationalize. They treat crime when it deals with Hispanics in one fashion and when it deals with Anglo perpetrator, they deal with it in another fashion.

A White news producer in Albuquerque also said the coverage is uneven, especially when it comes to crime that occurred in the city's South valley, a predominant Hispanic area where he lives.

> We cover crime in that area and there's a perception that the South valley is riddled with crime. Truth of the matter is statistically, the northeast heights where most of the whites live and the middle class lives, that's where most of the violent crime occurs in Albuquerque. But the only time they see the South valley on the news is when there's been a drive by shooting or there's been somebody stabbed by somebody else at a barbecue. So you know that's kind of the way it works. I live in the South valley and I love it and it's great. I don't have any problems. But watching it on the news will give you a different perspective or a different idea.

A Chicana producer at the station saw a qualitative difference in how crime was covered, depending on the geographic location of the crime. She argued that if a murder occurs in the South valley, it is a 1- or 2-day story, but if it occurs in a White part of the city, more attention is paid to the victim and to catching the perpetrator.

> I think that sometimes when there's a murder in the Northeast Heights, which is predominantly white, some people jokingly call it

White Heights because it's mostly Anglo people, but whenever there's a murder there, its not supposed to happen there. And we'll go out of our way to find out who that person was, who that family was, why it is happening there. If there's murder in the valley it's a voice over and nothing else, and this happens time and time again. If it was Joe Local who died down in the South Valley it was probably a gang member and that's the end of the story.

Her station's crime reporter agreed:

I think for the most part where I think the media as a whole really fails the Hispanic community is in crime coverage. What I tend to see really fall through the cracks are murders that tend to be drug or gang related. We tend to give those a little less intense coverage than perhaps some other murders for various reasons.

I think we're guilty sometimes of not down playing, but not playing up certain murders when we do it for others and what part of town where it happens and what motivation may be, i.e. drugs has a lot to do with it.

In Hawai'i, most of the concern over crime coverage centered around coverage of indigenous South Pacific Islanders. A Samoan social worker, who hosted a cable access program, said he saw patterns in coverage in regard to crime:

I think we Samoans over here are somewhat neglected in terms of reporting, and I really don't understand why. Only when something is bad, will they cover it. Something bad meaning a murder case or a house beating, a wife beating or spouse beating or domestic abuses and all that. But as far as positive issues relating to the contributions made by the community, I think reporting is poorly done.

The news director at the station studied in Honolulu offered this in way of an explanation:

There are some times it seems to me that a lot of our crime stories are about Samoans and Tongans. But these are the crime stories that seem to be more like the spousal abuse or child abuse, where they've come from a culture where it's not unusual to be very physical with

their mate or their child. They don't deal very well with tempera-
ment and relations among themselves all the time. They'd just as
soon settle something with a fist fight than with a discussion or con-
versation. But I don't think it's, I mean its never struck me that, you
know, we're being unfair to any particular race or people of color.

According to the Hawai'i Commission on the Status of Women, sta-
tistics do not indicate higher incidents of spousal or family abuse
among Samoans or Tongans than any other group.

Gutiérrez (1980) found that often times Hispanics were treated
in newspaper articles as "problem people." Entman (1992) found in
his study of local coverage in Chicago that "the images of blacks accused of crimes appear to be different from those of whites," and
that in general, portrayals of Blacks made them to appear threatening.

Why is this significant? Gray (1987) put it this way:

> What is presented and omitted from the news implicitly establishes
> (and reinforces) perceptions of the appropriateness and naturalness
> of the existing moral, political, and racial order. The news media
> tend to support (through their selections, framing, omissions, pre-
> sentation) groups, institutions, and activities that embrace the en-
> during values of society—capitalism, assimilation, individualism
> and social order. To the degree that groups and activities are ex-
> cluded or framed as deviant and illegitimate, such framing helps to
> establish public definitions and terms of social discourse. (p. 388)

When news makers continually choose to include images of people
of color as perpetrators of crimes and omit images of people of color
as normal citizens, they reinforce the idea that people of color primarily exist outside the bounds of legitimate social behavior. As a
culture, Gray argued, we know what not to do by watching the
news, and the people participating in the deviant acts are often
there with darker skin than the White norm. In discerning what stories will be covered and how crime stories will be presented, news organizations send out messages about where crime occurs, and what
crime is routine and what crime is out of the ordinary. As indicated
earlier, nightly mention of murders and robberies in certain areas

adds to the belief that certain areas of a city are unsafe. But none of these crimes may be covered in extreme depth, because crime is expected—is the norm—in the poor and segregated areas of the city.

By giving extraordinary coverage to a crime that occurs in a more upscale, White neighborhood, the message implicit is that crime is this area is unusual and rare. Or it may even send a message, in the case of coverage of a murder, about the relative value of a victim. If murders in the "bad" part of town are routinely covered by only a brief mention in the news, whereas a murder in the "good" part of town is treated with a splash and more in-depth story, newscasters may seem to be making value judgments about the relative worth of human life.

The assignment editor in Albuquerque asserted that his police scanner was color blind, that all crimes were reported by the police dispatcher without mention of race-ethnicity. This, on its face, seems a strong argument. But to make this assertion one would have to know whether the police presence is the same in all areas of a city, if all groups within that city report crime at the same rates, and to what crimes police themselves decide to pay close attention. As well, calls issued by the dispatcher to patrol cars often do include the address of the crime or complaint, and scanner listeners know what those addresses mean. One address indicates the Chicano neighborhood, another means a predominately White neighborhood. Addresses carry with them references to sections of town, which also represent certain racial-ethnic composition. A crime near the country club may well warrant a different response from news organizations than a crime in the poor part of town.

Again, there is evidence here that suggests that in at least these two news organizations in these two cities, crime coverage may be reinforcing hegemony by reinforcing inscribed ideas about who commits crime (people of color), where most crimes occur (communities of color), and where crime should not occur (White, affluent neighborhoods).

The news director in Albuquerque acknowledged his station was probably not doing all it could to cover communities of color, but he had an easier time articulating the problems he had seen working in television news in his home state.

I think we could do better. There are questions in my mind about how well we cover them. It's something that being from Minnesota with a very large Native American population, that's something that's always bothered me. How we tended to cover it or how they, how they got to the top of the news pile, in this case with Native Americans it was with Pow Wows or protests. And you know, is that a good mirror on the community? I don't think so. Where those things are stories, I think there's something in between there.

## ISSUES WITHOUT COVERAGE

If coverage of racial-ethnic communities tends to be centered around cultural celebrations and crime, that should mean there are other substantive issues involving these groups not being covered by local television news stations. Community leaders had no trouble naming a myriad of issues that receive little, if any, coverage from the local television news operations.

Jim Baca is a former TV news journalist who ran for Governor of New Mexico and served 2 years in the Clinton administration. He does not believe the local television stations cover the Hispanic community to any extent.

I don't think they cover it. Probably because their staffs aren't in tune with it and their news directors and their producers. Most of them didn't grow up here, live here. There's a lot of stuff going on in the West now. Incredible stuff. There is epic change going on in the West. And everybody sits by and lets it go by. They don't even know what's going on. You look at this city and what's happening in Rio Rancho, see what's happening with natural resources and water supplies. It's just totally ignored. Just missed the boat.

What Baca is referring to in Rio Rancho, a community just outside of Albuquerque, is the site of the development of a huge, new Intel plant. Although the plant itself had received extensive coverage, several community leaders pointed out that few stories had been done about what potentially negative impact this large industrial development was having on the environment and on natural re-sources.

Richard Moore is a community activist who has tried to focus media attention on issues like environmental racism, but, with what he says, is little success. Moore said there are a host of issues the local media do not touch upon, including development in Albuquerque.

> I'd say gentrification. The whole issue of relocation and dislocation. With the expansion of downtown there's a need for more parking, more space, and there's new people coming into the area, and it's our community that's being impacted.

> Education is another. They're talking about building a $25 million dollar high school in Rio Rancho and saying that it's too bad that kids are going to school in barracks. It's really too bad, but have they done any coverage on how many years our children in the valley have been going to school in barracks? We have year-round schools here. Half the schools where our children are going don't have air conditioning. And you talk about hot, in June or July.

The growth issue seemed to be a key problem in New Mexico. Albuquerque television can be seen through the state, there are only a few other, smaller stations in the state, so Albuquerque stations are responsible for covering an extremely large area. Santa Fe, the capital, is just over an hour from Albuquerque, and is experiencing phenomenal growth. So much so that property taxes had increased over 800 percent in recent years. Yet, during the time spent in New Mexico, there was only one television news story done at the station focused on growth issues. In a newsroom computer archive check of stories about growth over a 6-month period, only 21 stories were found that mentioned growth or development. In contrast, there were 91 stories found that mentioned Indian gambling, a phenomenon that was relatively new in a number of New Mexico pueblos. And in even greater contrast, there were 293 stories found regarding the trial of a Native American accused of killing an Anglo woman and her children in a drunk-driving accident.

Debbie Jaramillo is the mayor of Santa Fe. She is critical of the local television stations' lack of coverage of growth issues, not just in Santa Fe, but in the entire region.

Even Northern New Mexico, if they just want to focus on Northern New Mexico, not just Santa Fe, I think there are a lot of great stories on what growth has done to this part of the state and to the Hispanic population. There have been growth problems that have impacted the Hispanic community, our indigenous population and I don't think enough attention has been given by the media as to how we're going to solve it.

In regard to Native Americans in New Mexico, as was indicated earlier, gambling received extensive coverage from the station observed in the study. But what did not receive as much coverage, were other stories taking place on the state's many pueblos and reservations. But by simply looking through Native American newspapers that put out regional editions, one could easily see the number of stories that could have been covered. During the time I spent in New Mexico, stories that could have been done by the local station might have included: Hopi tribal leaders, with a threat of a federal injunction, allowed to go onto Navajo territory to gather eaglets and red-tailed hawks for use in ceremonies; the loss of native language on some reservations and efforts made to preserve it; or cuts in the Bureau of Indian Affairs' budget that could impact local Pueblos, including cuts in new housing construction, remedial education, adult education job training and employment programs. During this period the *New Mexico Business Journal* offered a special center section with 11 articles on different business and economic issues concerning Native Americans, including profiles of successful Native American businesses. Instead of stories on the interesting and varied business interests of these groups, the television stations instead ran stories emphasizing primarily casinos and gambling. But even in gambling stories, there were issues below the obvious that were not being covered. During a visit to a New Mexico Pueblo I discovered that Tribal officials had started a program to use gaming money as seed money for small business grants, and several small businesses unrelated to gambling had begun as a result of this program. According to tribal officials, the program had received no media coverage.

Community leaders in Hawai'i also reported that there were a number of issues not being reported by the local television news organizations. Jim Anthony's organization had been involved in a legal battle over pollution of wetlands and streams on Oahu. How well did the local television cover the issue?

> Poorly. Like it does lots of other things. I mean there has been sporadic interest. You know one of my major criticisms of the news industry, in particularly the visual medium which is so important, is that they have done very little to cover over and above the usual 5-second, 10-second, or 20-second, half-a-minute soundbite. They've done very little to cover anything in depth. So people get very fragmented pictures of what's happening. Not only fragmented, but confused and confusing pictures of what is happening. That's one of the sad things about the visual medium in Hawai'i. That it follow the way news is reported on the mainland. And so the reportage on this particular issue of major pollution on the windward side has been fairly meager.

Haunani-Kay Trask, a scholar and community activist who watches local media closely, states:

> For a long time they've never talked about the terrible health conditions of many Hawaiians. Now they occasionally talk about it but they don't connect it to historical causes. For example the diet. It's not why we can't eat what we used to, it's what we eat now, we eat bad food. Never mind the fact that economically we can't grow our own food or harvest it from the sea because we no longer control those means.

Undoubtedly the biggest issue concerning native Hawaiians and perhaps all people living in Hawai'i is the sovereignty issue. The word *sovereignty* and exactly what it means as a political issue changes dramatically depending on what group one speaks with. For some, it means return of all power to Native Hawaiians, and a dissolution of the American authority over the islands. To others it means at least a more equitable balance of power between Native Hawaiians and others, in regard to issues such as control of Native Hawaiian lands. To still others, it means the formation of a separate Hawaiian government, such as the form of government Native Americans currently have in their reservations and Pueblos. At the minimum, sovereignty is a very politically charged and complex issue. The local television news stations had covered the issue, with increasing frequency, as was self-reported and also according to community leaders. But what came into question was the quality of that coverage. For example, of the many different sovereignty groups and different leaders, who did the media cover most often? One group in particular practiced routine civil disobedience, with members setting up their own sovereign encampment. This group formed its own justice system and issued subpoenas for various public officials. Such activity was difficult not to cover, because it provided many elements that television news thrives upon, such as conflict and visual spectacle. But other sovereignty leaders felt such coverage did little to aid in the public policy debate concerning Native Hawaiians' rights. Sovereignty leaders, such as attorney Mililani Trask, said the depth and breadth of the issues are not routinely covered.

> It tends to be pretty much sensationalist. You can definitely count on the fact that cameras will be there if it's a demonstration and they anticipate something like traffic is going to be disrupted. The more you can accommodate television, their coverage is going to be better. But I think this a more difficult, complex issue. It's hard to get everything across because they're looking for a short soundbite.

Kaleo Patterson is a pastor who has been active in the sovereignty movement and is part of a coalition of clergy and churches that support sovereignty. He reported that he and others have often been left out of coverage because they didn't fit the mold of activist.

> The movement is not just a wild-eyed, angry, psycho Hawaiian who hates Christians and that has been the depiction of the movement. But there are churches involved, there are pastors involved who have been speaking about the morality of the issue but the media, for whatever reason, is very resistant to that more balanced image of us.

Even within the Honolulu TV station, some acknowledged that not enough had been done to try and cover sovereignty adequately. A White reporter, who is a native of Hawai'i, saw the station's coverage as superficial:

The Hawaiian sovereignty movement has been very much covered, but maybe there's a tendency to just get into the trap of covering whoever comes across as the loudest or the biggest, and therefore that's the one you always call for the interview. Whereas the voices of sovereignty are myriad and really, they should be, you know. Why always take one extreme element and have him, always give him the right to be the spokesperson for all these people? And yet because of the laziness of the press and because he's always available to give a quote they'll do it, so I think we fail there.

But an Anglo anchor thought the station had done a good job.

I'm happy with it, I'm happy with our coverage. I think if we did any more we'd be overplaying it because my personal take on it is that there are not many people in the state that give a damn.

I just don't have a strong feeling for that at all. I just, I can appreciate their ancestors' feelings; you want to honor those traditions and that culture, I have no problem with that. But to deny we're part of the United States of America, or that we shouldn't be, I just, I can't ... I don't buy that and it just doesn't ring any chords or strike any bells with me.

The station's news director also felt that the station had covered the sovereignty issue well, but did not believe it was an issue that was crucial to most people living in Hawai'i.

I'm well aware that Hawaiians think that they have been terribly screwed, but you know, what I do not accept is that it's my fault or the fault of any other people here now. We're talking about wrongs that occurred 200 years ago, 150 years ago, and I don't think it's any more my fault about those terrible things than it was my fault about slavery.

## Hegemony and Incognizant Racism

It should not be surprising that, to people from the mainland United States and even to Whites who have spent considerable time in Hawai'i, the sovereignty issue does not seem to be a particularly important issue. Whites are the colonizers of Hawai'i and as can be seen in many other settings, colonizers often have a difficult time understanding their role in history or even sympathizing with the colonized. That these sentiments are also reflected in daily news practice should not be surprising. But in this study, it provides one of the more dramatic examples of hegemonic control of the public discourse. The fact that the stations continually fail to provide comprehensive coverage of an issue, which may threaten the continued profitability or even existence of local television stations, is evidence of the imbalance of power between normal citizens and news media. As was discussed earlier, none of the stations are locally owned, let alone Hawaiian owned. All are held by large mainland media conglomerates. In the newsroom observed, there was no policy banning coverage of the sovereignty movement, yet little in-depth coverage took place. The news director and others were not particularly sympathetic or interested in covering the core issues raised by the sovereignty movement, such as what is the role of the United States in colonizing Hawai'i, or what rights do or should Native Hawaiians have in regard to controlling the islands?

The only policy that banned coverage was an unwritten rule concerning the station's consumer coverage. The station had, for several years, offered consumer reporting as part of its coverage. They offered viewers a station phone number they could call in to for help, or to complain about products or services. Yet it was well known among newsroom staffers that the station would not cover any complaint concerning automobile dealers. Why? Three different newsroom employees explained that it was simply because car dealers were some of the stations' best and most consistent purchasers of advertising time. In other words, automobile ads were crucial to the profitability of the station, and no negative reporting of car dealerships was allowed. Of course, this unwritten policy was not publicized; no disclaimer was run on the stations' newscast saying, "Call us with your consumer complaints, unless it has to do with an automobile." So viewers were led to believe the station news staff would look into any complaint—about a toaster oven or Chevrolet minivan. But in truth, the only consumer journalism that took place concerned only products other than cars or trucks.

If journalists in the station were not willing to do reporting that threatened the station's advertising base, how much more willing might they be to aggressively report on an issue such as sovereignty, which could eventually raise questions as to the rights of White corporations to do business in Hawai'i? In other words, if the station already had in place a practice that excluded stories about influential advertisers, is it any surprise that little substantive coverage was offered of an even more threatening and radical topic such as sovereignty?

Within the newsroom, people to whom I spoke knew about the "no car coverage" policy, and seemed to understand that it posed ethical problems; yet, seemingly no one was willing to take on the issue. So, although the policy directly impacted only one reporter, the consumer reporter, in daily practice, there was an implicit consensus that existed among all journalists who worked in the newsroom and they allowed the policy to continue unchallenged. The same kind of dynamic can be applied to coverage of sovereignty or to coverage of people of color. Some reporters try to cover the issue, others realize more should be done, still others do not even have that level of awareness, yet all work together each day to produce a product that consistently excludes stories about entire segments of the viewing audience. This process can be called *incognizant racism*. The practice results in racist coverage that is a distinctly different kind of coverage of people of color than exists for the White population. For the news workers I encountered, both in this study and previously, the systematic exclusion of coverage of people of color was not necessarily an intentional act, yet it still occurred, resulting in racist coverage. To call this neglect "unconscious" raises questions of Freudian intentionality. That is why *incognizant* may be a better descriptive term for the phenomenon. *Incognizant racism* may be a manifestation of Essed's "everyday racism," in this case applied to daily news practice.

This phenomenon was not limited to Hawai'i, but also took place, as we have seen, in Albuquerque, and also took place in other newsrooms where I have worked, and included myself as an unwitting participant. *Incognizant racism* gives us a way of conceptualizing how news practice consistently may miss the mark when it comes to coverage of people of color. At one level, it may be the result of a reluctance to cover issues that directly threaten the continued existence of the *status quo*. At another level, it may simply be a lack of awareness, due to years of cultural training in White, middle-, and upper-class norms and values, that excludes a world of issues outside a reporter's consciousness. As Essed's "everyday racism" concerns the process that takes place in daily experience, *incognizant racism* is a term I propose to describe this process in news practice where journalists consistently neglect to cover the issues and complexities of communities of color.

*Incognizant racism* occurs when journalists produce news products day-in and day-out that simply exclude any meaningful coverage of racial-ethic communities. In some cases this may actually be a conscious and intentional act, but at least in the newsrooms I have observed, it is not an overt process. It is the result of dozens of daily decisions, of years of training and practice, of decades of cultural orientation, and of a well-documented history of systematic and institutionalized neglect. It is both an individual and collective process. In the newsrooms I observed, neither news organizations as a whole, nor the news workers as individuals had the desire to change coverage to be more inclusive.

If people of color are not important to us, if people who are different than ourselves are of little concern, if issues crucial to communities of color never penetrate our psyches, if these communities and these issues are not even a faint blip on our personal radar screen, then we are destined to make decisions, write stories, put together newscasts as if people of color don't even exist. We will construct newscasts that are filled with pink faces and stories that are interesting and amusing and important only to other people with pink faces.

# Chapter 3
## Access

*There is too much media in too few people's hands and they have to much control over content.*

—Jesse Jackson

Many factors may contribute to the poor news coverage of people of color in the communities studied. In addition to the inability of some news managers to conceptualize and integrate coverage of people of color into daily news products, there is also the other side of the news coverage equation. That is, the people who desire coverage, in this case Mexican Americans, Native Americans, Native Hawaiians, Japanese Americans, Chinese Americans, Filipino Americans, and all the others who have ancestry from a host of other countries, as well as those whose racial-ethnic background is not easily defined, whose lineage represents a myriad of different cultures and race-ethnicities, may not have access to the newsroom?

## KNOW-HOW AND ACCESS

People inside and outside of the newsrooms studied had strong opinions about whether people of color in particular had the opportunity to muster up news coverage when it was desired. We have already seen that communities of color reportedly are getting coverage when they are involved in crime or engage in a particularly visual cultural festival, but what exactly happens when members of the community need to get word out about an issue or an injustice? Civil rights worker and community organizer Ray Armenta reported little success in getting attention for issues.

> I'm very involved in Hispanic organizations and countless times we will contact the media to cover some of the stuff we're doing; by and large everything we do is proactive, positive for the community. Whatever we're doing—scholarships, civil rights—it's active, it's good, you know what I'm saying. And we call, as early as last month we called, and we had a convention and we wanted some coverage and we got zilch. I mean we didn't get any, and no, no they don't cover enough of that.

Syndicated newspaper columnist José Armas has written columns about people and ideas that were offered to, and turned down by, local television. Armas said it is difficult for an everyday person to get the attention of the local news stations.

> I think people who are persistent may be able to get an audience, but it's like an uphill effort to get that story. If it doesn't fit into a certain definition of what's important to them, they tend not to hear, it's difficult. It becomes difficult for other people to get their story out and in some cases activist organizations, for instance, there is a tendency to kind of dismiss them until they do something really dramatic or whatever. There's kind of, the door's not closed but it is tough to push the door open.

Michael Guerrero heads an organization fighting environmental racism. His group recently held a news conference to talk about issues concerning growth and development in Albuquerque. When none of the local TV stations showed up, his group staged a protest at two of the stations that are located across the street from each other. Members of his group were able to meet with representatives from both stations, but Guerrero reported that after those meetings little changed; it was still difficult to get the stations interested in issues concerning development and its negative impact upon people of color. At the station I observed, Guerrero was considered to be an outsider and did not hold much credibility with news staffers. As Armas mentioned, quite often activist groups are simply dismissed. If the consensus in the newsroom is that the *status quo* is good, that social conditions are generally acceptable, then such activists may have little chance of finding an audience in newsrooms.

Yet several people at the stations I observed, including this assignment editor in Albuquerque, believed their newsrooms would welcome any story ideas, despite the source.

> I believe the newsroom is very accessible to everyone because they can just call or they can fax or people can even stop by. Yes, I would say the newsroom is very accessible to anybody who wants to come in or call or fax.

A reporter in the same newsroom expressed a similar sentiment:

> If they call the assignment desk, it doesn't matter what your accent is, if the story's a good one we're going to cover it. If you ignore Hispanic stories, for example, if you mistrust the Hispanic people for some reason, you'd be stupid to start with, but you'd also be shooting yourself in the foot because that's a huge percentage of our state's population, and their problems and their lives are newsworthy a lot of times, you'd be cutting yourself off from the people in the state if you did that. So I think our newsroom is accessible.

Of course, to an extent, these news workers are right. Anyone can drop by a television station, anyone (with the means to buy the equipment) can fax a story idea or announcement to a news operation, and anyone can call a newsroom (although with automated answering systems they may not get to speak with a live human being). But the question that remains is what will happen to your suggestion, to your phone call, or to your fax?

An assignment editor was a bit more realistic in his assessment of the chances of a viewer's suggestion actually becoming a news story.

> They can look in the phone book and call the television station, but I don't think enough people understand when they call, why some-

thing is important. And to them it's a very important matter. It's a very important issue. But when they realize, they don't realize they are competing with a very limited, even though we have four newscasts, when you chop everything out and you have your news blocks, when there's a certain amount of time, and there's some stories that are so significant that they're going to be repeated once or twice, they are competing against other stories. And people don't realize they've got to sell a person like me.

A news producer put it this way:

> There's a problem of exactly knowing how to get access for any group of these folks. Most folks don't understand how the process works and that presents a barrier for any charity or you know any volunteer group or anything. They just don't understand. They think their event is as worthy as any other but they just don't sell it the right way.

A Chicana news anchor said she did not feel most people in the community had the training to know how to sell a story to a news organization.

> I think there needs to be a lot more education about how you get a story on the air, put together a press release, put together some kind of a hook, know how to sell the story, how to add relevance to the community as a whole, not just a segment of the community, know that there are visuals involved. I think that this community does need to catch up with others in learning how to pitch a story and get it on the air. There are a few out there, organized groups, but as a whole, no. They just call up and say there's something going on, will you cover it? And they're disappointed and there's a lot more that goes into getting a story on the air and selling it.

Selling a story means being able to convince news workers that there is something current and newsworthy about an event. It means convincing them that there are visual elements to the story that make it more interesting and visually appealing to viewers. But there is no set of criteria that guarantees coverage. News values vary from market to market, from journalist to journalist, and may even vary from time to time, depending on how much other news is available on any given day. Most of those interviewed in the newsrooms agreed though, that being able to sell a story—convince news workers of its relevance—would increase the possibility of obtaining coverage.

## PUBLIC RELATIONS AND ACCESS

Although everyday citizens may have no idea how to sell a story, professional public relations firms offer clients that expertise. One clear example of how to sell a story well occurred during the time I spent in the Albuquerque newsroom. The Albuquerque Convention and Visitor's Bureau organized a media blitz that surrounded a week long group of activities based on the idea of promoting economic and cultural exchange between the United States and Japan. The week included a conference on world trade, workshops and demonstrations of Japanese culture, exhibits and performances, banquets and even a ribbon cutting ceremony to kick off the week. Among the extensive materials sent to the local newsrooms was a glossy-covered file folder full of pre-written news releases and public service announcements, an extensive calendar of events, and summaries of each event, including names of press contacts with phone numbers. A graphic artist had designed a colorful logo for the event. A number of other printed pieces arrived each day through the mail; these were followed by phone calls and daily faxes to the newsroom as reminders.

In response to this well-coordinated event, the Albuquerque newspaper and television stations offered extensive coverage throughout the week. The station I observed had pre-produced a series on Japanese–New Mexico relations pieces that aired each night on the 10 p.m. news, and this was augmented by daily coverage of one or more of the day's scheduled events. What is interesting is that this was not breaking news, nothing in particular had changed or was new about Japan/U.S. relations, but the coverage was largely in response to the carefully orchestrated and professionally designed campaign aimed toward local media. One could argue that some of the events may have indeed been newsworthy, such as a visit and speech by the vice-president. But the coverage went far beyond that speech and included stories about Japanese art, dancing, and food. On one level, the coordinators of the event were playing to traditional coverage patterns; ethnic cultural events that were very visual. But without the professional media relations, it is highly doubtful that coverage would have been nearly as extensive. Although one might argue that this constituted an opportunity for coverage of people of color in Albuquerque, i.e., the Japanese-American community, there was nothing about the conference itself that addressed the particular issues that might be crucial to local Asian-Americans. Instead, the focus was on the economic gains that could be found with continued relations with Japan.

Local newsroom journalists, including the Albuquerque news director, admitted that the professional coordination of events for Japan week influenced coverage decisions.

> We, the media, we get used and some people really know how to use us, what buttons to push. And you know, that shows that we're only human. There's probably people that, that won't have access because they don't know how to use us. Hopefully we can be better journalists than that in that we can see beyond that, but we aren't always and probably aren't most of the time.

People who do not have economic power can ill afford to hire public relations firms, let alone pay for the design and printing of expensive press packets. To a news photographer in Honolulu, it boils down to an issue more about economics than it does race-ethnicity.

> I think there's a lack of knowledge of how to get it (coverage). I think there's a lot of people that's trying to do grassroots campaign with no money that doesn't know how to work it, they don't have any P.R. background. So they don't have the same kind of coverage. I think it's a money issue more than anything else, I don't think it's a racial issue. You know, you could have a Caucasian or haole that has a cause, but if he doesn't have the right public relations talk to it, he'll get shut down just as much as anybody else.

There seems to be a clear distinction between who may or may not get access and therefore coverage, when it comes to local news in at least these two markets. If people are not well trained and experienced in the methods of news decision making, chances are diminished for getting the local news media's attention. And in some cases, such as with Michael Guerrero, even if you are experienced and know how to call a news conference and know what to say in a news release, if you are perceived as outside the norm, as radical, or beyond what news decision makers have decided is acceptable or credible, your chances of getting access are also diminished.

Also, if you do not have the economic resources to hire a public relations firm, you may find it difficult to garner news coverage.

## RETICENCE TO GAIN ACCESS

There is another aspect to access and coverage that needs to be considered. There are stories that may deserve coverage that involve groups and individuals who do not actively seek publicity. Native Americans interviewed indicated that they almost never call media organizations to tell them about events. They may see no reason how coverage, which in the past has often been negative, would be beneficial to them. They are not alone.

> I'm sort of surprised that given the coverage on Hispanic affairs, the Hispanic community hasn't done more about it. It's not just the TV stations who are sort of ignoring what's going on, how often has the Hispanic Chamber of Commerce gone over to the general managers and the news directors at the TV stations and said, listen you got to cover some of this stuff, you got to pay more attention to it. I don't think they have. (Jim Baca)

There are others who are reticent about trying to get coverage. Chinese-Americans Sai and Selina Yeung own several business in Honolulu. During an interview they indicated they would have a hard time imaging the circumstances under which they would ever call a television station and solicit coverage. This is despite the fact they are active in their community, and there are issues they are concerned about.

Q: Do you think people in the Chinese-American community would go to the TV station and tell them?
Sai: Oh, no.
Q: Why not?
Sai: You see, especially the Chinese people, we are the kind of people that is, shall we say, conservative? There is not anything is only happening to us. With exposing things, we are not the type, especially it seems, like we are guests in this country.

The Yeungs, though they have lived in the United States for a number of years, still feel reticent to contact the media about problems they might have. If television news organizations are waiting for viewers to come forward and provide them with news stories, this may be an expectation that may never materialize. Even when people do come forward, they may be ill-prepared in the nuances of selling a story to an assignment editor who may not be particularly interested or well informed about what they might be saying. An assignment editor in Albuquerque admitted that "I often times shy away from covering a story that affects certain ethnic groups simply because I may not totally understand the issue." So a number of factors may affect access that people of color have to news decision makers, including their own reticence.

## JOURNALISM AND ACCESS

Newsrooms seemingly are open organizations. It's not difficult to find a station's phone number, fax number, mailing address, or e-mail address. But there seems to be a significant gap between being able to call a local news station and to successfully have the station cover and televise a story about an event or issue. To successfully persuade news decision makers to dedicate time and resources to a story requires a good working knowledge of how newsrooms operate and what values may be important to local journalists. But even with that knowledge, coverage is not guaranteed. Several of the community leaders interviewed were media savvy, with knowledge of details such as what time of day is best to hold a news conference, or how to write an effective news release. Yet this still did not guarantee coverage for these individuals and the groups they represent. People without this expertise may have an even more difficult time getting media attention. Those groups, however, who have resources to hire public relations firms and are trying to garner coverage for more mainstream types of news, say the promotion of a Japan-America week, had much more success. Joseph Turow (1992) wrote " ... the mass media tend to uphold the legitimacy of the established economic, political, educational, artistic, religious, and military organizations of the society" (p. 153). What was witnessed in these newsrooms in regard to access supports a hegemonic model of mass media, wherein those with power and legitimacy and extensive financial resources in the culture have better opportunities to get across their ideas to a mass audience.

Most discussions of journalism ethics include the idea of completeness, whereby journalists do their best to include a full account of all the basic information in a story. I have argued before (Heider, 1996) that if certain segments of a community are not covered, it is difficult to argue that journalists are giving readers or viewers anything close to a complete story, no matter the topic. In this case, because citizens did not have the knowledge or financial resources needed to sell a story, or because they were reluctant to seek out media coverage, or because the local media decided simply to ignore certain stories, people of color did not have ready access to news coverage.

# Chapter 4
## Geography and News

*… the three and a half millions of square miles;*

*The eighteen thousand miles of sea-coast and bay-coast on the main—the thirty thousand miles of river navigation,*

*The seven millions of distinct families, and the same number of dwell- ings—Always these, and more, branching forth into numberless branches;*

*Always the free range and diversity! always the continent of Democracy!*

—Walt Whitman

From where you sit right now, how close is the nearest television sta- tion? If you live in a city, especially a major city, you are probably not far. But that's not the case with all Americans. Another access issue concerns the physical location of the television newsroom in rela- tion to the communities that news workers cover.

In television, local stations are concerned with A.D.I. (Areas of Dominant Influence), also known as D.M.A. (Designated Market Area). What both of these terms refer to is: where people can pick up the stations' signal, where people can see the station on cable, or defining who are the stations' viewers. With new technology, this is not as clear cut as it once was. But with both stations studied, there is a fairly well-defined coverage area. In both locations, the entire state constitutes the station's coverage area. But do these stations actually cover the territory that makes up their respective state? How does geography impact coverage and access to news coverage?

## NEW MEXICO

For Albuquerque, the D.M.A. includes at least the entire state of New Mexico. There are smaller stations in Roswell and Farmington, but several of the stations in those cities are satellites of stations of Albuquerque. For news coverage, the studied station considered the entire state its news territory. Even though the station had affiliate stations in two smaller markets that served as bureaus, that still left a large part of the state without any news presence close by. If a story warranted coverage (e.g., a high-profile criminal trial, a disaster of some type, or a political scandal), then the station would have to send a crew, or pay a part-time freelance photographer (stringer) to shoot some video that would be shipped back to the station. But stringer fees and sending crews to remote areas are both costly. That meant for day-to-day coverage, rarely was news reported from such remote locations. It becomes a formula of convenience and of audience strategy, not only because the corners of the state are remote, but also because they have a relatively low population compared to the Albuquerque metro area. Therefore towns in the west such as Gallup, in the southwest like Deming, in the northeast such as Questa or Raton, and cities in the east like Nara Visa, see little, if any, routine news coverage.

One assignment editor was frank in categorizing his station's coverage as limited generally to counties in the immediate area.

> We concentrate in a four-county area, being Bernalilo, which is Albuquerque, Valencia County which is south of us, Los Lunas and Belen, Santa Fe County and Sandoval County which is directly north of us, the town of Bernalillo and Placitas and Rio Rancho. Those are the areas we primarily serve, and if we don't report about those people they're going to think that, well, state news is interesting but we would like to hear what's going on in our town. Now my

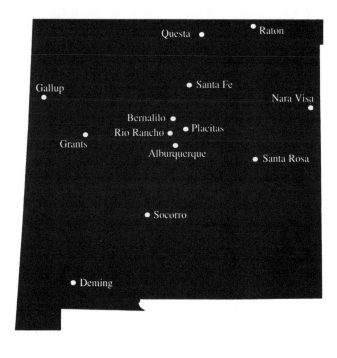

Map of New Mexico

concern is, that it's conceivable, it's at the expense of Grants, Socorro, Santa Rosa to the east about 100 miles from here, and many, many, many other towns.

The assignment editor understood well that his job was to make sure the news of Albuquerque was covered first and foremost, next came news coverage in the four counties he described. After that, there was a sharp cutoff of news coverage. So, as he put it, at times the news of the metropolitan area gets covered at the expense of news in smaller, more remote towns and communities. A reporter in the Albuquerque newsroom knew someone who worked on a Navajo reservation in a remote part of the state. When he visited there, he was struck by the fact that things happen there that can go completely unnoticed by people in Albuquerque.

> I just wondered about that, what if something's going on out here, how do we ever find out about it unless it is of such catastrophic nature that the ripple is felt and we respond. Something like the Junta virus scare that made news. But there may be all kinds of other things going on out there.

What this constitutes is a form of *geopolitics*, where distinctions are made about stories based on their location, how important that location is to the viewing audience, and how difficult it may be to get to and from that location. On the first level, news workers may ask if their viewers care about what goes on in the more remote locales. It seems there is a scale of importance, depending partially on the other news of the day that may be competing with that story. Also taken into consideration is the relative interest in the story itself; the more unusual or devastating the story is, the better the chances are that a crew might be dispatched. But this is just the first step in this complex (but often quickly executed) cost-benefit analysis. Next comes the assessment underlying many decisions, which is that the majority of the viewing audience is not in eastern New Mexico, nor in a remote Pueblo, but in Albuquerque. If news workers are most interested in finding and reporting news that impacts the majority of the audience, then there is less chance the station will send a crew to cover news that takes places in remote locations that are isolated from most people in the metropolitan area.

Finally, there are the economic considerations. It is time consuming and costly to cover stories in remote locations. First, there is time spent by the news crew; often it will be mean overtime pay because of long travel time. Next, to get videotape back from a location in a timely matter, a station may have to dispatch a satellite truck, which may mean paying overtime to at least one more person, a technician or engineer, to get the truck to and from that location. Gasoline must be paid for, satellite time must be purchased, meals and hotel costs may figure in. Even if a stringer (a part-time employee) is contracted with to provide the footage, freelance fees are often expensive, plus there are the shipping fees or satellite costs to get the tape back to the station.

All of these factors combined often mean that coverage of remote areas is rare. The level of importance a story must have to receive coverage is significantly higher than that of a story within a short driving distance from the station. Herein lies the problem.

In New Mexico, according to the U.S. Census Bureau, most of the Native American population does not live in the four counties covered most often by the Albuquerque TV station. Pueblos and other Native American lands are scattered across the state, in some cases far removed from the metropolitan areas. Cibola County, for instance, has one of the largest Native American populations in the state, where the Indian population makes up close to 40% of the county's population. Cibola county is in the northeast part of the state, not near Albuquerque or any television station newsroom. All people, but especially people of color, who live in locations geographically removed from Albuquerque, face some serious barriers in getting news coverage.

The stations have no reporters or news gatherers in these locales. This also decreases the chances of news coverage. It results in a kind of geographic hegemony. Although news workers do not reject outright any story idea from any place in the state, because of the factors just discussed, the chances are greatly diminished for stories to be covered in less convenient areas. Therefore, the result is more stories about people and events in close proximity to the station. There is no outright discrimination against those who live an hour or more away from the station, yet, because of these constraints, those with stories or perspectives who live outside the local area suffer from a lack of coverage, and their perspectives are rarely represented in the mainstream discourse of daily news.

## HAWAI'I

In New Mexico, no matter the distance, towns and villages are still reachable by car. Yet Hawai'i offers a different set of challenges. At the Honolulu station, the coverage area includes the primary populated islands including O'ahu, the island where Honolulu is located,

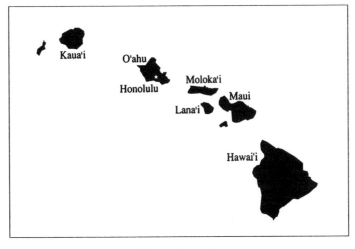

Kaua'i

O'ahu

Honolulu

Moloka'i

Lana'i

Maui

Hawai'i

Map of Hawai'i

as well as Kaua'i, Moloka'i, Lana'i, Maui, and the big island, Hawai'i. Other than Oahu, news workers are faced with crossing the ocean to report on events on neighboring islands. The station observed for this study maintained no news bureaus on any of the neighboring islands, even though the islands of Maui and Hawai'i both host relatively large populations. Honolulu still has by far the largest population base, including the center for the state government. The mayor of Kauai, Maryanne Kusaka, was clear about how much coverage her island receives:

> We really get limited coverage from Honolulu. Primarily, if we have a significant issue pertaining to the environment or in relation to recovering from recent storms or if it may be a confrontational issue perhaps between the legislative bodies on the island, then they come over and do the interviews.

An Episcopal priest who is involved with the Sovereignty movement reported that he had tried to encourage the stations in Honolulu to provide more coverage on the other islands, but with little success. He and others met with station news managers to discuss coverage.

> We talked about being able to get news in this area (sovereignty) from the neighboring islands on a timely basis. A couple of them acknowledged that they had no bureaus, but of the couple of them, only one has improved any today. But they acknowledged they have no way to get video from the neighboring islands, but they can get voice in. They can fly somebody to film the neighboring islands in here but they have no way to get direct feeds. (Tom Van Cullen)

A news manager at the Honolulu station acknowledged that coverage of the neighbor islands was insufficient.

> We're not covering them as well as we should. One reason is a problem with the sources. In order to get people over there and get our pictures back is very expensive. One of the stations opened up a bureau on other islands and that didn't work out. They cost a lot of money, to keep people over there and it costs a lot of money to hire freelancers over there, it's just difficult to do. Even though, geographically, they are not that far away, getting there is expensive. Keeping people there costs money and we, you don't do as good a job with coverage with the neighboring islands as we should because we are licensed to operate on those islands. We have a license on the big island, we have a license on Maui and our market is the entire state and Oahu gets the lion's share of coverage. Sure when there's a big fire, crime, some big spot news gets coverage, but we don't have a reporter who is able to take the time that is necessary to really get in and do major coverage of stories. It's becoming a matter of economics.

An ocean adds to the remoteness of neighboring islands.

Therefore in Hawai'i, coverage remains centered around a geographic mainstream, that is events and people that are located on O'ahu. It is certainly well within the technological capabilities of the stations to set up bureaus on neighboring islands and send video stories back either by microwave or satellite technology. Yet, managers have decided not to, based on similar rationale to that of the managers in Albuquerque, who must be persuaded to send crews to remote locations in New Mexico.

The majority of Native Hawaiians, like the majority of people in Hawai'i, live on O'ahu, in Honolulu County, which covers the entire island. But in Honolulu County, Native Hawaiians only make up a little over 10% of the population, according to U.S. Census Bureau figures. Native Hawaiians make up a larger percentage of the population in each of the surrounding counties, ranging from 15% to 40%. Thus, on these neighboring islands, where there remains more native influence and a larger percentage of native peoples, there is less coverage. Many of the people active in the Sovereignty movement live on the neighboring islands. Most of the physical territory of the state exists on the other islands. But crews do not get to most of these islands daily, let alone even weekly, to report news.

The physical, geographic, and financial limitations take a toll on coverage. One reporter noted that such isolationism creeps into more than just coverage decisions, but also the way in which reporters and producers report and write the news.

> I catch things. For instance, when people say "city council" that bothers me because I think they should say "Honolulu City Council," because I think it's arrogant for us to assume everyone knows we're talking about Honolulu. I mean, the poor people in Kaua'i, Maui, and the big island have their own city councils and if we're going to talk about the Honolulu City Council we should that. I don't think we should say "Mayor Jeremy Harris." I think we should say "Honolulu Mayor Jeremy Harris," because they have mayors on other islands also. I think geocentricism is pretty common, especially when you have a barrier like water.

The physical geography not only has affected coverage decisions, but also the very way in which news workers frame stories. By not using qualifiers like "Honolulu" when talking about the Honolulu City Council, the message being sent by the station is clear: When it comes to news, Honolulu and O'ahu are the center of all important activity in Hawai'i. Anything else could be considered secondary, less important, or outside the mainstream. Night after night when stories are about events and activities only on O'ahu, the same message is sent.

## CULTURALLY CONSTRUCTED GEOGRAPHY

Water may not be the only coverage barrier in regard to the area covered by the news stations in Honolulu. One reporter lives in Wainae, an area that is a 45-minute drive from downtown Honolulu and is populated primarily by people of color, especially Native Hawaiians and other Pacific Islanders. It is widely believed to be a poor and more dangerous area. She felt that the area is often excluded from coverage, unless it is crime coverage.

> I would like to see a lot more (coverage), I mean from all the stations. I would like to see more positive publicity on my side of the island. I mean Wainae has had a bad reputation as far back as I can remember, and that's the one thing we haven't been able to lift out. It just doesn't stop with, from murders to riots in the schools, no one ever forgets, you know. Wherever I go people say "you're from Wainae?" and it's just kind of sad to see their reaction.

Wainae is not all that far from the station, but because of negative perceptions of the community, it was constructed as a very remote place. But it was the newsworkers' and news decision-makers' attitudes more than actual physical geography that made Wainae remote.

The question raised here is, how do attitudes that consistently favor one area over another affect coverage? In both Honolulu and Albuquerque, from reports inside and outside the newsroom, there is a clear demarcation between stories that take place close to the stations and stories that do not. Among news workers there are boundaries to news that might determine if it is covered or not; some boundaries are based on distance, others are based on perceptions of areas, such as Wainae.

Reporters in Albuquerque were reluctant to visit or learn about activities taking place in Native American Pueblos. Some of those Pueblos are located within a 30- to 40-minute drive from the city. In other words, they were physically close to the station, yet in regard to coverage, they seemed geographically remote. But it is a culturally constructed remoteness, not one determined by actual distance. As a number of geographers have discussed (Gregory, 1994; Sibley, 1995) there is a human element of geography that is impacted more by social conditions and perceptions than by actual geographical factors such as topography or distance. "The human landscape can be read as a landscape of exclusion," writes Sibley. In the case of the newsrooms in Albuquerque and Honolulu, there is a landscape of exclusion, and it includes not just locales that are physically remote, but also locales that have been excluded because of social and cultural factors, that I would argue include race-ethnicity. Both Wainae and the New Mexico Pueblos are populated with native peoples. Both are constructed as remote by newsworkers.

## NO REMOTE NEWS

Geography then, whether physical or socially constructed, may offer barriers to access, reinforcing the idea that most news represents the mainstream perspective. One can also talk about decisions made to cater to the majority of viewers, the ability of sources to represent the *status quo* perspective, and the location of those trying to tell a story. It may be helpful to think of local news, at least in these two markets, as most often representing the center. What constitutes the center may depend on a number of different factors. For instance, national and state capitals rarely actually sit the geographic center of a territory, nor do the world's largest cities. But they do represent the center of activity, commerce, and even of thought. If we consider ideology for a moment, the *status quo* might also be thought of as representing the center of popular opinion. In this way then, those that represent remote news from remote areas or news that is considered remote or outside of the mainstream, may find great difficulty in getting their message across via local television news.

# Chapter 5
## History and News

*White man, hear me! History, as nearly no one seems to know, is not merely something to be read. And it does not refer merely, or even principally, to the past. On the contrary, the great force of history comes from the fact that we carry it within us, are unconsciously controlled by it in many ways, and history is literally present in all that we do. It could scarcely be otherwise, since it is to history we owe out frames of reference, our identities, and our aspirations.*

—James Baldwin

Access, then, may be influenced by geography and by the resources of those who are trying to get their message out. But as we've seen so far, physical barriers and even economic barriers may not be the only factors precluding people's ability to garner news coverage. It may also be that news workers' orientation to the world may also preclude some stories from being covered. No news event takes place in a vacuum, isolated from other events and influences. News is historically situated, it happens at a particular time, in a particular era. How that news is perceived may often be influenced by that particular historical era and also by the news worker's understanding of where that event falls into their bigger picture of the world. But to place stories in such context, means that journalists are making determinations about the current and historical relevance of each potential story. Therefore it is important to consider those news workers' racial-ethnic backgrounds or their class standing, as was discussed earlier, and also their knowledge and understanding of history. One might argue if a news gatherer has no understanding of the history of the area where (s)he works, this could greatly affect not only what stories may be selected, but once selected, how such stories are presented. If story suggestions from audience members do not jibe with news workers' understanding of the world, access to the news dissemination process may be limited.

## JOURNALISTS' KNOWLEDGE OF HISTORY

People of color in the communities studied had quite a bit to say about reporters' knowledge of history, especially local history. For instance, when José Armas was asked why he rated coverage of people of color as poor, he responded in this way:

> For one thing I don't think they know anything about us. I think that despite in New Mexico, for instance, that where we have a history of almost four hundred years, we have almost twice as many Hispanic governors that have served in New Mexico as presidents of the United States, yet very few station workers could name three Hispanic governors of this state. They don't know our language, they don't know our customs, they don't know our history. They don't know anything, they're not taught it in school. The schools don't make any effort to teach the history of the Native American and Hispanics and as a result we live in an ignorant society. And that's reflected in how the community is displayed or presented by the media, or television in particular.

Community organizer Ray Armenta agreed.

> They get out of college and they think that's all they need to know and there's a lot more to know about our state. There's a lot of history here. We were here before Plymouth Rock was founded, we were here before, I mean almost a hundred years before the Pilgrims landed. There's so much to us, how many people know we were un-

der the Spanish flag for 222 years and only 27 years under the Mexican flag? And it's most of these reporters that don't know any of this.

Native American attorney Kevin Gover said that while doing interviews, some reporters demonstrate their lack of basic historical knowledge.

> I mean they ask you questions that indicate a painful misunderstanding of how tribes came to be and what they are, the status and the powers that they have. I mean sometimes a reporter will even mispronounce a place name and you just kind of go, where have you been? It can happen to anybody but you just expect a little more of a reporter, a little more background before they start asking their questions.

Gover said he sees that lack of knowledge of reporters concerning Native Americans and their well-defined set of legal rights, based on years of negotiation and legal precedent. This legal history is often lost on reporters who are new to the area.

> Part of it is resentment and it's not constant, but the occasional resentment of the tribes really does come from a lack of understanding. "Why is it they get to do those things" and it's sort of classic when you are new to New Mexico, you sort of look around and say why do the Indians get to do this and the Hispanics don't or the Blacks don't? And that is so basic to us that it's hard to forgive that level of ignorance and yet you see it all the time. You see it less, frankly, in New Mexico, than you do in a state where there are no Indian tribes, nevertheless it's extraordinary how little some of these reporters know before they start talking to you.

A Native American anchor in Albuquerque also has noticed how little newsroom people know about local history, even if they are native to the region.

> I don't think kids growing up here have a good sense of New Mexico History, it's not a requirement. It's just not a required course which is upsetting to me. Just like there is no requirement in the schools to take Native American history. Or at least the understanding of diversity of the cultures that exist here in New Mexico. There's no re-

quirement for that. And it bothers me that people who come here for jobs don't become versed in, not only contemporary issues and contemporary players, but also on the history. Because so much of what happens, has happened here in New Mexico and you've got to know about it.

Author and scholar Hanuani-Kay Trask is interviewed for television stories frequently, and hosts her own cable access program. She has not been impressed with reporters' knowledge of complex issues concerning Hawai'i.

> I don't think I can name one person that I know in the television part of the news, that I would consider a serious, well-informed person. Not one. They do not read the books we write. They do not know the history. So when they interview you, it's impossible for you to explain anything to them because they don't know the reference points.

That lack of knowledge, the lack of a broader historical context, creates a barrier of sorts, between news sources and news gatherers. News workers who do not have a basic knowledge of the history that frames current events may have difficulty identifying and relating to traditionally disfranchised peoples who could offer much in the way of distinct and diverse news. The sources themselves may not trust the journalists who have continually demonstrated a lack of understanding of the most basic issues.

## BIG TURNOVER, LITTLE EFFORT

I was able to visit five Pueblos during the research period, and met with tribal officials on three different occasions. These officials reported that other than the one Native American broadcast journalist who was working at the station I observed, no local television reporter, to their knowledge, had ever come to visit the Pueblo to gather information, until a news conference was held, or a big event occurred, such as a tragedy. If reporters are not visiting tribal lands, if they are not spending time in the barrios, if they are not seeking out people and information from areas like Wainae on O'ahu, it would seem then that there is a breakdown in the news gathering process. People in these communities report they feel as if they have little access to reporters, because they never see or talk to them except under the most adverse conditions, such as in the event of a crime or natural disaster. One tribal administrator (Roy Montoya) put it this way:

> Something hot comes up, something happens today and they want to be first with the story and its kind of a rush job. And I always tell people you really have to get acquainted with Indian people before you can really report on some of the things that are being done out there on the reservation, you have to understand the people. There is a reason tribal governments do what they do, but there's a lot of people that don't take the time to study the subject before they report on it.

When it comes to covering any group of people, trust is an essential element in the relationship between a reporter and a source. When it comes to Native Americans, trust may not be easily established in a short amount of time.

> A tribe, because of our experience, does not forget. This is not something that has happened within 5, 10 years. A lot of things have happened to us for 500 years and it's very hard to go from one thing to another because of past treatment. By suddenly I don't mean a week or a month or a year even. It takes a long history, like if somebody does something to somebody, it takes a long time to build up trust. It doesn't just happen overnight. And overnight in the history of the relationship between non-Indian and Indians, overnight could be 30 years. (Roy Montoya)

This problem is compounded by the fact that turnover at most television stations is high. News workers change jobs quite frequently, often looking toward larger markets and better salaries once some experience is secured. Former news manager Jim Baca noted that there are very few people in television newsrooms over the age of 40, especially small- and medium-market newsrooms, and that means very little collective memory, even of recent history.

You just don't see it. It may be the one profession that you can think of where there's no old people working. And I think it's for various reasons. One, the pay level. And two, this infatuation with youth, you know, that you have to look good on television.

Question: What does that do to coverage?

It screws it up completely. You know these young kids that are 25, 26. I mean we were there, too. We were that age when we were doing this. They just don't have the experience. Perfect example, sending someone to city council, sending somebody to legislative committee meetings. They just have no clue what's going on. They see it on the surface, but they can't analyze it and see what it really means. If they stay on the beat for 2 years maybe they start understanding what's going on. They develop sources and all that sort of stuff. But it just doesn't happen. It's a constant rotating, revolving door.

Police information officer and community leader Mary Molina Mescall also said the high turnover of broadcast reporters is not helpful:

Reporters moving in and out of a community is a disservice to issues that affect people of color. That's certainly the case here, where the history is different from California or Texas.

And it often is not just the reporters who are moving in and out of the community. Turnover in the newsroom also includes photographers, producers, assignment editors, and news directors. This is a fact for people who deal with the news workers regularly.

I think there's a lot of transitions in these news departments. I've seen a lot of assignment editors come and go. A lot of times they're coming in from other places like Washington, D.C. or California and they're career minded and they're moving on to other places. So they're looking for as much bang for the buck as they can get. And not willing to take the time to immerse themselves into the community and understand what the issues are, who the people are, what the history and the politics and all the dynamics are that lead to an issue are. (Michael Guerrero)

Mark Santoki is the editor of the *Hawaii Herald*, a Japanese-American newspaper in Honolulu. He had also noticed the turnover in television reporters.

> Because going to events myself you see different reporters every single time. That's definitely a limitation because you don't get to know the people in the community and I think my analysis of it is that if you work here for a couple of months you'll notice the same people are involved in all those different things, I mean you're talking to maybe a dozen people who are community leaders and you know of, you build a relationship with them it gives you a good understanding of the community. It's something television should pay a little more attention to.

If reporters are coming and going frequently, this impacts news coverage.

## NEWS OF THE NOW

Community leaders reported that so much turnover adds up to news decision-making and news coverage that primarily is done from a here-and-now perspective. If a reporter knows little or nothing of what has taken place before, then stories are often treated as if history began the day the reporter arrived in the city. In the case of people who have been in the area for a 100 years or 500 years or longer, as is the case of some indigenous peoples, this becomes a crucial fact. For instance, when covering a development issue, knowing the history of events that led up to this moment may be crucial in the way in which a story is framed, even in making decisions as to who to interview and what information to include. Native Americans, Native Hawaiians, and others interviewed for this project reported that often they are not even called to speak on key issues about which they have been concerned with and fighting about for decades.

High turnover does not foster historical perspective. But the lack of historical knowledge is not just due to turnover. People also reported that broadcast reporters who had been living in a place for some time still did not take the time to learn and understand more about some of the communities they cover.

> I think in New Mexico here, there's been a core of reporters that have not learned over the years. It may not be their fault, they may be, they just may not be interested in it. Or they may not have seen it as important to their career. And it may not be, but certainly if you're going to cover issues of a population, you should know the population. (Frank Chaves)

A lack of historical knowledge makes it convenient for news reporters to construct a story, or a world view, without having to acknowledge entire groups of people or entire historical eras. For instance, a reporter in Albuquerque is assigned to do a story on legal gambling at a Pueblo. If the reporter knows nothing of the several thousand-year history of that tribe, if he or she knows nothing of the Spanish occupation of the territory, or the treaty agreements between the U.S. government and the Native Americans involved, how can the reporter help but write a story that omits this crucial context? If a reporter in Hawai'i knows nothing of how the Hawaiians existed on the islands for centuries, if he or she knows nothing of the colonization of Hawai'i, first by the British and eventually by the United States (including the military takeover of the sovereign government), and then is assigned to cover a story on the sovereignty movement, how could he or she possibly give full and proper consideration to all the events and context that has come before?

If, as it has been said, journalism is the first draft of history, it may a first draft without context or diverse perspectives. Because media is one of the primary sources for information in our culture, how that first draft is written may be crucial. Journalism without a sense of history in these markets may well be exclusionary and slanted toward people who hold power in the modern era, because of lack of access of those people who have different perspectives and information that is deemed outside the here and now.

# Chapter 6
## Conclusion

*If all mankind minus one were of one opinion, mankind would be no more justified in silencing that one person than he, if he had the power, would be justified in silencing mankind.*

—John Stuart Mill

What you have read in the preceding chapters contains the primary thrust of what people told me, people inside the newsrooms and people of color outside the newsrooms, as well as what I observed during my time in these cities. I would argue that these two newsrooms represent, in many ways, the local, daily method by which hegemony operates through local news. Coverage is denied to no one. Yet, for some, it is difficult to obtain. News workers have autonomy. But the decision-making power still lies in the hands of a few, who remain seemingly committed to supporting the *status quo*. Powerless groups are presented in newscasts, but they are often seen in stories framed by culturally-frozen norms, such as are seen in ethnic festivals, or they are associated with deviant behavior, such as crime. People of color are called upon as sources. Yet, because reporters do not have an adequate knowledge of the history of an issue, the sources' comments may be framed in a story that does not fully realize the complexities of issues. Stories, on occasion, do air that deal with an issue in a well-rounded way and that portray people of color as more than just stereotypes. But this is not the norm; many stories that are done still reinforce existing beliefs about people of color individually and collectively.

Howard Winant (1994) puts it this way:

> Hegemony is a system in which politics operates largely through the incorporation of oppositional currents in the prevailing system of rule, and culture operates largely through the reinterpretation of oppositional discourse in the prevailing framework of social expression, representation, and debate. (p. 29)

Based on reports from people of color in these two communities, the result in these newsrooms is that the preponderance of coverage still supports the existing sources of power in the culture, and that people of color, their ideas, their issues, their very images, are still framed primarily in ways in which they fit into traditional stereotypes or they are simply portrayed as outside the norm, if they receive air time at all.

## NEWSWORKERS

Both newsrooms studied were journalistically sound. These newsrooms were not (based upon my observations and my years spent working in and watching local news around the country) newsrooms where sloppy reporting and shoddy news gathering routinely take place. It was, in fact, quite the opposite. These newsrooms were filled with good broadcast journalists—smart people, some of whom had years of experience, and all of whom were trying to do a very good job of bringing viewers the news each night. In Hawai'i, the newsroom was filled with veteran reporters, most of whom had lived in Hawai'i, if not all of their lives, a significant portion of their lives. In this way this newsroom was unusual, as many newsrooms do not have this kind of collective background available to them. In Albuquerque and in Honolulu, the newsrooms were diverse, except at the top. The point I want to make here is that these newsrooms (again based on my time in over a dozen newsrooms in seven differ-ent states and on time spent working with nine other newsrooms through a Washington, DC news bureau) were not unusually bad news operations. They were, in fact, better than many I had spent time in. People in these newsrooms were proud of their news prod-uct and they worked hard in their news-gathering efforts.

Yet despite news workers' best efforts, I found consistently inade-quate coverage of communities of color. But perhaps more signifi-cantly, I believe I have been able to begin to identify some of the reasons coverage was inadequate, at least in these two newsrooms. There is no single reason. Lack of coverage is the result of a number of different factors, some of which I detail here.

First, news decision making in both of these newsrooms was not conducive to a pluralistic approach to news coverage. The power in both newsrooms resided ultimately in the hands of a few White managers. These managers, though well meaning, still consis-tently made decisions that reflected first and foremost their own values as to what was or was not important on any given day. As much as objectivity in journalism is discussed, many basic deci-sions about whether to cover a story or not are based on one or two people's personal, subjective judgments. Because neither news-room had overt sets of criteria upon which such decisions were made, it became obvious that managers used personal experience to make news decisions. People of color did participate in news meetings, did contribute story ideas, and did, on occasion, influ-ence news coverage. But as anchors and as staffers in other posi-tions, they exercise limited power over the daily news product. Even those people of color who were producers did not have final jurisdiction over what would or would not run in their newscasts. In these newsrooms there was no sustained commitment to cover-ing communities of color. No reporters were assigned to ra-cial-ethnic beats. There was a desire to be inclusive, but no way in which that desire was put into operation in day-to-day news prac-tice. Hegemony is evident in the practice of news decision-making that continually reinforces values and norms held by White man-agers who have no stake in radical change. Because most news-rooms across the country are still managed primarily by Whites, it is difficult to tell what impact an increased number of people of color in management positions would have.

News organizations should be making every effort to recruit and retain people of color in management positions, rather than so often funneling them toward more visible on-air positions. Part of this effort could begin with paid internships, which are rare in the broadcast industry. Such programs could target students interested in being producers and assignment editors, and could help groom a new generation of news managers.

But efforts cannot simply begin and end with recruiting. As we have seen, the problems that produce inadequate coverage in these two markets go well beyond the skin color of the people sitting in the news director's office.

There must also be a fundamental change in the way news workers conceptualize news. It is no longer acceptable to produce the majority of stories about people of color in narrative forms that continually frame them in terms of traditional ethnic festivals or as deviant criminals. These communities are filled with hugely divergent people, who work and live and love and struggle in the same wide variety of ways as do people in any community. In these communities there are dozens, hundreds, thousands of stories to tell. It is time, or past time, to go beyond the usual coverage of the Hula and latest gang-related shooting. There are many meaningful issues, such as development in New Mexico and sovereignty in Hawai'i, that deserve consistent and thorough coverage.

Using Essed's framework of everyday racism, I was also able to see how conditions exist in two newsrooms that produce daily coverage that consistently excludes the complexities and nuances of communities of color. Essed discusses in her work elements that come together to constitute everyday racism. Those elements include a *status quo* where dominant views are not questioned, a reluctance to admit and face racist behavior, and a reality based on existing social order. There were elements of all of these conditions in the newsrooms studied, prompting the development of a new term in regard to news practice, that of "incognizant racism." This is an attempt to explain the consistent behavior of well-meaning journalists who, apparently without intention, continue to participate in journalistic practice that systematically excludes meaningful coverage of people of color. News workers know there are important issues in the community, they know the sources they might interview about those issues, yet no (or few) stories are done. News decisions support dominant views, reality is defined by the existing social order, and the exclusionary decisions are routinely ignored.

## DELIMITATIONS

This study did not set out to produce broad, generalizable findings about the content of local television news programs. Instead, the idea was to spend time in two news operations in two of America's most diverse television markets, to try to gain a better understanding of why news practice fails to produce more comprehensive coverage of communities of color. Although some evidence was found that may help us as we try to understand news practice and how that practice is framed by larger social theory, this remains a locally situated study.

Perhaps a more serious limitation of the study are the qualifications and standpoint of the researcher. In qualitative research in general, and in ethnography more specifically, the researcher is the tool used for measurement. Therefore who I am, what I see, what questions I ask, how I influence people around me becomes part of the research I am doing. As a White male from a privileged class and racial-ethnic background, I perceive the world in ways that may not be shared by those whom I study. However, the focus of this research is not people of color themselves, but of the news organizations that are charged with covering cities that include communities of color. Because newsrooms are still controlled by-and-large by White males, ultimately I was studying people like myself. This, added to my own experience in newsrooms, shaped the way in which I have framed this project, and the way I have analyzed my data. On one hand, my background helped provide entreé to the newsrooms. When news directors and others met me, I was able to convince them in short order that I was "one of them." Even though I was up front about the subject I was investigating, coverage of people of color, there was, I believe, an underlying assumption by some that I would be sympathetic to the news organizations because of my news experience. I was and am sympathetic to the constraints, economic and otherwise, put upon journalists daily. But as is indicated in the study, I am less sympathetic to the result. In short, more must be done. My "whiteness" may have also had an influence upon those people of color whom I interviewed inside and outside the news- room. I did not perceive any reluctance, however, on the part of in- formants to speak freely, and I believe the frankness with which people spoke, as is evidenced in the preceding pages, serves as a ba- sis for judging whether this is a serious concern. It would be interest- ing, however, to see a similar study done by a person of color, to see how that researcher's perception might differ and how sources might relate to them differently in interview settings.

This study was also very much influenced by the members of the communities whom I interviewed. I selected a broad range of people with different titles, different racial-ethnic backgrounds, and differ- ent experiences. This was not, as was discussed earlier, a random sample. It was a constructed group of sources, and had the group been constructed differently, the results might have also been dif- ferent. Although I did interview people in the business community and people who work as part of government, I also interviewed many grass-roots organizers and people who might be considered system outsiders. Had the interview list been constructed primarily of institutional insiders, there might have been fewer complaints about coverage overall. For me, the consensus that was voiced by people from different racial-ethnic groups, with different class back- grounds, in different professions, in areas separated by thousand of miles, provided some convincing evidence as to some level of valid- ity with regard to what I was being told.

## FUTURE RESEARCH

As with any research, there are a number of questions this project raises. Among them are, how do people of color operate in news management positions? Does coverage significantly change when people of color control news decision making? Given the lack of coverage documented here and in other studies, what would an alternative news agenda look like? Is there a way to integrate traditional methods of selecting news with a more inclusive approach, and would this create meaningful change in the news product? Are news workers open to input from community members? Could building coalitions between news workers and community members result in more responsible news coverage of people of color?

Because of the dearth of research done in regard to people of color and broadcast news, and especially the lack of research on the news coverage of people of color other than African-Americans, almost any additional research would be helpful in aiding our understanding of these and other questions. Perhaps this lack of research is revealing in itself, giving us a clue about a bias within the field of communications research and our own role in supporting the dominant social order when it comes to asking questions concerning race-ethnicity.

# Chapter 7
## Possible Remedies

*The acknowledgment of our weakness is the first step toward repairing our loss.*

—Thomas A. Kempis

*Society is made up of groups, and as long as the smaller groups do not have the same rights and the same protection as others—I don't care whether you call it capitalism or communism—it is not going to work. Somehow, the guys in power have to be reached by counterpower, or through a change in their hearts and minds, or change will not come.*

—Cesar E. Chavez

Given what's been described in this book thus far, what, if anything, can be done about it? Columnist José Armas had this overview:

If television provides a portrait of what a community looks like, television needs to understand that the portrait of the Hispanic and Native American is right now a distorted picture and whatever it is that they would do to provide a reflection as they do with the Anglo population that is exactly what they need to do with the minority population, who are the majority in this state. Right now there is a distorted picture of our community being reflected and so to put it in a simplistic way, that is, what has to happen is that the negative aspects of the news is a part of, where we play a part, but also we play a part in the positive aspects, the constructive aspects, the leadership aspect, the values, the contributions. Those reflections are not in focus. Those reflections are either absent or distorted.

It is questionable whether any media outlet can ever provide a true reflection of any community. But, certainly, news organizations can make efforts to try to be more reflective than is currently the case.

## REPORTER OUTREACH

Ideas for how this might happen came primarily from interviews outside the stations. This is not surprising because for news workers to have thought through suggestions on how coverage might improve, they first would have had to wrestle with the idea that present coverage was somehow inadequate. Only one veteran reporter, who had recognized inadequacies in coverage, suggested a first step toward improving coverage.

> We have far too few people in the field. We probably have the same number of people in the newsroom, or we have more people in the newsroom than when I first came here, but they're all in the station, they stay here. They're producers, they're assignment desk people, we have three times as many anchors now as we used to have, our manpower is all inside the newsroom.

> The people out in the field are a smaller force than there was 13, 14 years ago. I think that's alarming, because sitting around a desk isn't the right way to cover news. We're desk-people heavy and we're field-people light and that's wrong and there's an imbalance that should be fixed.

This reporter had seen his station add newscasts and add staff and add to the budget. But, he reported, the thing that the station had not added were people who are out in the community finding and reporting the news. From my experience, it is not uncommon for stations to add newscasts and add producers and anchors to staff those newscasts but not to add reporters and photographers to gather material for those newscasts. It is cheaper to use stories from feeds from the networks and CNN than it is to hire more reporters to report on the local community.

People of color in these two communities had no difficulty coming up with suggestions on how coverage could improve, and they tie in with what this reporter said. Community organizer Michael Guerrero said he would like to talk with reporters on a more regular basis.

> They need to have, I think, some system of outreach. I think they need to have some kind of a staff person, or a reporter, however they want to set it up, to go out and just meet with people. Sit down with organizations in the city and say: "What are you doing," you know, "What's interesting, what kind of issues would like to have covered?" They should be tourists.

Samoan Loia Fiaui said he thinks televisions station's "negligence is due to a lack of understanding, the lack of involvement between the Samoans and news media, or the news media and the Samoan community." At the Honolulu station, no reporter was assigned to any ethnic community specifically, including the Samoan community. In Albuquerque, no reporter was assigned to cover the Hispanic or Native American communities. Native American attorney Kevin Gover said having a reporter assigned to cover the community would be helpful.

> Every media outlet ought to have some sort of relationship with each tribe. At least make the approach and say we'd like to talk to you about how we cover things, when we have a question, who should we talk to? Just to establish protocol for communication and that would improve things a million percent. Part of that would be to encourage tribes to think about how they want to deal with the media, what things are happening on their reservations that they could have gotten the media interested in, and to teach the tribes how to deal with them. When you have a reporter trying to sneak around ten ways trying to get the information they want, it's not only annoying, it shatters trust between the tribe and the media, and I think if you had that

protocol in place, the media would almost immediately get the information they are looking for.

Tribal administrator Roy Montoya agreed. "You know Indian tribes hire people, mostly lawyers to help them deal with the non-Indian world, the non-Indian world, as far as I can see, rarely does that."

## EDUCATION

As was discussed earlier, often everyday citizens may be unprepared to call a news station and successfully pitch a story idea. News organizations could help in this area, for instance, by holding training sessions for people who want to learn more about how news works and what would make a successful strategy for selling a story to a news organization.

As much as this might help, most community members interviewed for this study indicated that education would be helpful, but not just education of community members, but also the inverse; community members helping to educate the media. That was community organizer Richard Moore's suggestion:

> It would seem to me that there should be some training of staff when they come into a community, into a city, state, or whatever, in terms of what the cultural realities are here. And that should be something that the station should accept responsibility for, setting up training for its staff people. It should be across the board, not just the news person, but the managers, all of those people who are not out here everyday, but they're making some kinds of decisions for the station, they should be involved, too.

Moore suggested taking news workers on a tour of the community, with the hopes of changing some perspectives. "Just go on a tour with us and try to understand what we've been talking about from a different perspective of people who have been here for generations and generations." Fiaui sees the relationship developing into a kind of partnership.

We want to invite them out to the community, we want to let them know of our community so that we can know each other on a partnership level. So that we can have open access to them, likewise them to us. So it creates sort of a continual dialogue between us and them. So that if they want, say every so many weeks or every so many months we will cover this community. At least they could have some people here who can contact us and say, what's going on? Or we can just call you up when we have things that are worth reporting and news.

This was not happening at the time of the study.

Because they don't understand us, they tend to be very suspicious or since we don't know them we are afraid to approach them. Many of our people don't speak English very well so they feel ashamed to call or to go ask because they don't know how to relate in this society. They don't have the sophistication to make the presentation. But once we have developed some sort of open policy, once we develop some sort of contacts and nurture that relationship, and maybe some day put some of our children in as apprentices—training to learn about the media, to learn about TV, and maybe, who knows, one or two people working at the station from our community will improve things a lot. I think that will be one of the greatest services the TV people could do for us.

## Bridging the Gap

Education is a process that might open a dialogue between stations and communities of color, whether it's the station trying to educate the public on how to get a story covered or whether it's community members taking time to educate journalists about local history and current concerns.

Chicana leader Mary Molina Mescall, who deals with local media regularly, said she could see potential benefits from such an exchange.

Bring in someone to do some education about who we (Hispanics) are in New Mexico. What do we look for when see the news media come out? Try to be open, knowing that the community is going to come out with some really unreasonable requests, but get the dialogue open.

Environmentalist Jim Anthony was thinking along the same lines:

> We ought to be brave enough to bring in some really bright, articulate, smart people in to advise the media. To provide a sounding block. No matter how outrageous some of them might be. I mean, I'm not suggesting we bring in people who are from the loony fringe, but you know, good, bright people who have something substantive to contribute. And to meet regularly with the kind of people you're talking about, I think that would be the beginning of wisdom.

In fact, such exchanges had already taken place in Hawai'i, not with local television, but with the local newspapers. The *Honolulu Star-Bulletin* and *Advertiser* had started a program in which the papers recruited people of color from different communities to come monthly to the newspapers' office for a meeting with reporters and editors. Committee members spoke with the journalists about anything they had on their minds. They also served as sources for stories, allowing reporters and editors to broaden their range of sources. Also, committee members served in an advisory role. For instance, when one of the newspapers was going to run a particularly sensitive story about a certain racial-ethnic group, they faxed a copy of the story to a committee member. The journalists were not turning over editorial control of the story; they were instead asking these advisors to check the story for accuracy and to advise them if the story was offensive. Loia Fiaui served on the committee.

> I look them over and I say no objection or I can say, this story needs to be changed, or, in my opinion, this is not right. And whoever is doing the article will take time to talk to me and maybe some other people from the community, to further explain and define the implications of this upon the group it represents. So, I think it's a good start for the newspaper. I think the media, the TV should somehow look into that, if they can consider it. So that we

can work, more community leaders and more community people with some understanding of this issue to provide improvement of TV.

But not everyone in Hawai'i thought the diversity committee was a good idea. For instance, the news director at the station I studied reacted this way: "Oh, I'd never let them touch a story. That's the nuttiest thing I ever heard of." This reaction is revealing for a number of reasons. There are a number of people outside of newsrooms who try to control editorial content of stories, for instance sources who want to review a list of questions before granting an interview, or others who want to review and change a story before it is published or broadcast. This might explain why the news director and other journalists might react strongly to the idea of letting someone review a story before it airs or is printed. But allowing outsiders to review a story before it airs is not necessarily giving them control of the story. News workers would be asking for input and advice, but the control would still remain with the news organization. But by allowing community members a chance to review copy, a news organization is, in a way, just practicing good journalism. Traditionally, two parts of the journalistic ethic were that stories be balanced and complete (Klaidman & Beauchamp, 1987; Pippert, 1989). By allowing people of color to review stories, a journalist is taking a step to help ensure the story is indeed balanced and complete.

Diversity committee or not, most of the community members I interviewed suggested some kind of exchange of ideas between stations and the citizens. There was a strong sense that the broadcast news organizations were not particularly open nor interested in what people in the community had to say. This lack of openness, the lack of exchange of ideas, is something many of the community leaders mentioned, and they talked with hope about how that might change.

We need to be ahead of the game, in a sense, rather than being reactive. Far too many of us here are possessed with a flawless sense of how to be very careful, how to be so modest that we never do anything that is, that amount to living on the edge of a knife. I think it's a dearth of ideas, the dearth of ideas that the moguls of the media industry don't want to face. And I hope somehow or other this kind of cross-cultural fertilization would make people in the media, or at least one of them, I'd like to see one of the television stations break away from the other two and begin to set a new course. And you know, in human affairs, the way that you do that it seems to be, is you engage in creative discourse. You try to infuse people with ideas. (Jim Anthony)

If we really want to talk seriously about coverage becoming more complete and inclusive, change would need to occur on many different levels: from the employee at the foot of the organizational chart to station owners to the Federal Communications Commission (FCC).

Congress and the FCC, in the midst of deregulating the broadcast industry, have created an atmosphere in which increasingly fewer and fewer companies own more and more television stations. This, along with other changes, including the elimination of incentives for selling stations to minority owners, has decreased the likelihood that people of color or minority businesses will own or operate television stations.

For positive change to be truly top–down, the first priority must be to create a business atmosphere where minority ownership is possible. At the management level, significant strides would need to be made in hiring and retaining people of color as general managers, station managers, and news managers. As discussed earlier, the latest numbers on diversity in management offer little in the way of encouragement. Even worse, there are some indications that the numbers of minority managers have leveled off and may begin dropping.

But behind all the numbers comes something more basic: attitude—the attitude managers' project and the environment they create. There needs to be not only racial-ethnic diversity, but a commitment to diversity and coverage of diversity at every level. Reporters, photographers, writers, producers, editors, and managers need to be recognized when they do a good job of being more inclusive, when they work to ensure coverage is truly more complete, fair, and balanced. Managers need more deep and textured knowl-

edge of the communities in which they live. Reporters and producers can expand their rolodexes to include people of color as experts
on almost any topic. Producers can create stylebooks suggesting
how to avoid stereotypes in words and in images. News staff can do
everything from reading local history to visiting and/or moving to
communities they are unfamiliar with. Some new lines of communication might be opened if news workers would even consider simple
things like the places where they shop, eat, get hair cuts, or
work-out, and start doing these things in less familiar neighborhoods. These are hardly radical suggestions. The bottom line is
news workers, news organizations, owners of news organizations
have to be interested and involved in entire communities, not just
in the activities and events and lives of people who look like they do.
The future of local television depends on it.

Local television news organizations are faced with increasing
competition and a decreasing audience. With the advent and success of regional cable news operations and with the proliferation of
news sources now available via home computer, future success of local TV news is likely to be linked with its ability to convince viewers
that it is in touch with the local community. In these two locales,
people of color who in some way or another represent large segments of the populations said these local stations were clearly out of
touch. If that continues, the segments of the audience made up of
people of color may be lost once and for all.

# Appendix
## Detailed Methodology

In this study a combination of methodological approaches was utilized. In their book on qualitative methodology, Denzin and Lincoln (1994) discuss the researcher as bricoleur.

> The qualitative researcher-as-bricoleur uses the tools of his or her methodological trade, deploying whatever strategies, methods, or empirical materials are at hand. If new tools have to be invented, or pieced together, then the researcher will do this. The choice of which tools to use, which research practices to employ, is not set in advance. (p. 2)

Through this approach a researcher is free to respond to events and circumstances that arise in the field. This is not to say, however, that there should not be a methodological plan in place that will allow data gathering leading to answers to the research questions.

## PARTICIPANT OBSERVATION

For this study, ethnography seemed an appropriate starting point, or at least some of the methods of ethnography. For through the techniques of ethnography, a researcher may begin to see and understand the inner-workings of local newsrooms. Any ethnographer will be faced with what Geertz (1973) has described as "a multiplicity of complex conceptual structures, many of them superimposed upon or knotted into one another, which are at once strange, irregular, and implicit, and which he must contrive to somehow first to grasp and then to render" (p. 10). But, from spending time observing and interviewing, structure may emerge from the chaos. A newsroom has its own organizational culture, and within that culture, if one is to believe Ruth Benedict (1934), there exists a consistent pattern of thought and action. Although many ethnographers spend a minimum of a year or more in the field, I spent 5 weeks in each of two separate locations. Unlike many ethnographic studies, in this case the field was a place I was quite familiar with, having spent 10 years as a television news photographer, reporter, producer and manager.

Having a sense of familiarity with the surroundings offered both advantages and disadvantages. There were many things I was able to understand and adapt to quickly that someone who was unfamiliar with television news might have struggled with. For instance, I already had a good understanding of the hierarchy, the operating systems and politics of television newsrooms. This knowledge is something another researcher would have to spend weeks or months becoming familiar with. From my first contact with each news organization, this experience was extremely helpful in building bridges with the people who worked there. For instance, my experience helped pave the way to gaining entrée to the settings. Part of my ability to gain both news directors' trust was based on the fact that I worked in the business for a number of years and could address their concerns about the research.

In both of the newsrooms, acclimation came very quickly. There was almost an immediate sense of familiarity, just because of the many days I had spent working in newsrooms not unlike these. My experience also helped provide me with a reference point upon which I could begin building relationships with news workers. A memorandum was posted in each newsroom explaining who I was and discussing my news experience. Armed with this information, people in each newsroom would often begin discussions with me based on my past experience, and in some cases, we had mutual professional acquaintances.

But experience in the setting can be disadvantageous as well. I also brought with me into the setting assumptions and expectations formed during my years in the news business. There was a tendency initially to assume certain policies were in place or certain decisions were made in a way I had been familiar with in the newsrooms where I had worked. This was not always the case.

Because in any ethnographic research, the researcher is the instrument, prior knowledge can be problematic. But participant observation is not an objective method; it is instead, by its very nature, subjective, and so to try to construe it as something different may even more problematic. As Adler and Adler (1987) have written:

> The membership roles approach to field research calls on us as researchers to integrate and use our multiple roles in gathering data in the same naturally occurring ways we do in our everyday lives. We should not artificially bifurcate ourselves for analytical or scientific elegance. Our goal should be the integration and full use of ourselves as simultaneously, complex human beings with unique individual biographies and trained and dedicated researchers. To meander through our various roles (to different degrees) over the course of our research is not a grievous error, but a natural human phenomenon. (p. 86)

The goal, then, is not to completely divorce ourselves from who we are and what we know, but instead to draw on our backgrounds in an effort to get closer to members and the behavior we are studying. The balancing factor is the ability of the ethnographer to have perspective on his or her own work, trying to constantly stand back and reflect on what biases he or she brings to the field. So it was crucial for me to continually step back and reexamine basic assumptions, especially about decision making in each newsroom. Six years away from the television newsroom, in addition to extensive reading, thinking, and writing about news practice, also helped in providing me with a fresh and more critical perspective on issues which earlier in my career would most likely have gone unquestioned. When I re-enter a newsroom now, my viewpoint has changed considerably.

One advantage my experience brought to this study was my ability to understand news language. I have a good understanding of the jargon involved. As Spradley (1979) has pointed out, language shapes much of the setting.

> Language is more than a means of communication about reality: it is a tool for constructing reality. Different languages create and express different realities. They categorize experience in different ways. They provide alternative patterns for customary ways of thinking and perceiving. (p. 17)

Whether informants were talking about "soundbites," "stand-ups" or "uplinks," my past experience provided me with a knowledge of the jargon necessary to understand what was taking place in the setting. I already had an understanding of the symbols and referents that one might find in any one of a number of different news organizations. Although each setting provides its own variations, there is a set of understood conventions. How those conventions affect coverage will be discussed further.

I also brought with me to this study my own race-ethnicity and my own ideas about race-ethnicity. As a White male I must be aware of my own background of White privilege and how that impacts my view of the world around me. To conduct this study without that awareness would be to leave out an important aspect of the research. Instead of attempting to be invisible as I wrote about this research, as many ethnographers and other social scientists have done in the past, I have decided instead to place myself within this text, thus the use of personal pronouns. In this case, knowing who the researcher is and how that researcher fits into the process is crucial for an understanding of how the data are gathered and from what perspective data are analyzed and ultimately presented. To do otherwise would be to try to artificially mask an important aspect of data gathering and analysis.

As it turned out my "whiteness" was not necessarily a detriment in understanding perspectives from informants with different ethnic backgrounds. Yet this study is primarily concerned with a world of television news that is still dominated by White males. In that respect, it helped me in assuming the role of an insider, in order to offer an inside critique of this world. For the outsider's critique, I must depend on informants who can offer varied and unique perspectives.

I entered two news rooms in a peripheral membership role. Adler and Adler (1987) have outlined this role in some detail.

> Researchers who assume this role feel that some sort of membership is desirable to gain an accurate appraisal of human group life. They seek an insider's perspective on the people, activities, and structure of the social world, and feel that the best way to acquire this is through direct, first-hand, experience. They interact closely, significantly and frequently enough to acquire recognition by members as insiders. They do not, however, interact in the role of central members as insiders. (p. 36)

For 5 weeks at each site, I was in the newsroom each day. I participated in news meetings, interacted with news workers, accompanied reporters and photographers to stories, but was not a functioning member of the news staff.

As a newcomer to the setting, and as someone who was identified from the start as a researcher, there was always the chance of causing what Adler and Adler (1994) have called observer effects. That is to say, people may act in certain ways or say certain things to either try to please or displease an observer. This effect is a very difficult thing to gauge. I could have had more control of the trajectory of my visit by not disclosing the actual topic of my research. For instance, I could have simply told people in the setting I was on hand to study news decision-making. Yet I felt that to enter these settings under false pretense, and then later to write and publish about issues specific to race-ethnicity would be less than forthcoming. By being honest and direct, I was provided the opportunity to be myself, in most cases. Whatever news workers understood of the reasons for my being in the setting, it seemed that my behavior on a day-to-day basis was important in informants' decisions as to whether or not to confide in me, as other researchers have discovered (Wax, 1977; Whyte, 1955).

Any entrance into a setting, even a covert one, will cause some effect. Ultimately I could never justify in my own mind anything but a straightforward approach. Having said this, it seemed (as much as I could have been able to judge) that people were fairly open in sharing with me a wide variety of opinions on the station's coverage of people of color. Crucial to this was an awareness of how and where interviews and other less formal conversations took place. My more formal, taped interviews took place in isolated areas in the stations, often outside the building or in a conference room where we could not be overheard. Even more casual discussion usually took place outside of earshot of others. The place where I did observe my impact was in several newsrooms discussions about race-ethnicity that took place while I was on hand. Although I did not initiate these discussions, it seemed obvious that my presence and my interviews had caused some news workers to begin questioning the station's news practices, especially in regard to people of color. It was difficult not to participate in these discussions, but during them I tried as best I could to remain outside these discussions, trying instead to listen to others' ideas about coverage in general or specifically about a particular issue. If I had not done this, I might have been classified, at times, as researcher as advocate. For at least a brief time, my very presence may have caused some news workers to rethink the norms of their own coverage decisions, although this was not my express intent, at least in the short term.

My goal was to befriend informants and gather as much data as possible, but this still left me open to running the risk of misrepresenting myself to people in the newsroom. Fine (1993) has written about how ethnographers often fall into the trap of telling lies in research settings to reach certain objectives. One such lie is appearing so friendly, or so sympathetic, that those one is studying begin believing that your research will support their point of view. Although I tried to enter the setting with an open mind, much of what I knew about local news came from years of experience in newsrooms. Upon reflecting back upon those years I realized that when it came to news coverage of ethnic communities, something was missing. So, like all researchers, I entered the field with some expectations. Therefore, although I was in many ways sympathetic to the stresses and pressures put upon news workers, I was also aware of certain deficits that may exist in the way in which news organizations cover people of color. I knew that my findings might not highlight the newsrooms involved in the most positive light, and in fact, could potentially be highly critical of news gathering practice. Thus, as I entered the field I tried to be cautious not to intentionally misrepresent myself. I tried to make it clear that I held common beliefs with people because of my journalistic background, yet I tried not to offer many opinions about whether I felt news coverage of communities of color was or was not adequate. If I was asked directly I replied that I would not be studying the subject if I felt that there was not room for improvement.

Observations became an important part of collecting data in this project. As Denzin and Lincoln (1994) have observed, "qualitative researchers are more likely than quantitative researchers to confront the constraints of the everyday social world" (p. 5). Often because of these constraints there are things that are not or cannot be articulated by informants. This is when the researcher's observations become essential.

> As an ethnographer, your involvement in personal relationships with informants and your participation in community life will provide you with rich information to evaluate interviews. As time goes on, you will begin to learn about idiosyncratic and systematic differences between informant accounts and actual events, and it will largely be your observations that enable you to do so. (Agar, 1980, p. 110)

In both newsrooms, I was able to position myself at desks near the assignment desk, the area where most discussions take place and often where decision-making occurs. It is the center of activity during the day. Given this physical position, in addition to my inclusion in daily editorial meetings, I was able to observe most of the articulated rationale behind news decision-making. I was also able to observe interplay between news workers, helping me gain insight into the institutional structure of each newsroom, which also impacts daily news decisions. In addition, through asking questions and making other observations, I was able to discern other institutional patterns

such as news beats, a journalistic convention where certain reporters are assigned certain areas for continued coverage. These include
such areas as the police department, the courts, the city government, and the state legislature. The areas selected for beat coverage, the individuals selected for these beats, and also which areas
are not assigned a beat reporter, all influence the news process. As
in the case of the beat system, by combining interviews with observations, a researcher may begin to draw some conclusions concerning meaning of events that take place.

## INTERVIEWS AND TEXTUAL ANALYSIS

There are other methods of collecting data that proved helpful as
well. I had access to daily news scripts, as well as memos, through access I was given to the newsroom computer system. These, plus
newsroom handbooks and posted newsroom policies, also were
helpful sources of information. As Ian Hodder (1994) has written:

> Such texts are of importance for qualitative research because, in
> general terms, access can be easy and low cost, because the informa-
> tion provided may differ from and may not be available in spoken
> form, and because texts endure and thus give historical insight. (p.
> 393)

That is not to say that these texts contain meaning in and of themselves. The meaning comes in analyzing why they are written, how
they are read, and what each document means to news workers.
They become part of the larger picture the researcher is piecing together with other data. Other documents such as policy statements,
newspaper articles, and other background materials were also provided by informants inside and outside of each newsroom. Although most of this information was helpful primarily as
background material, newspapers, for instance, also provided some
interesting texts for comparison with the actual television news
content, helping me make determinations about coverage of communities of color.

In addition to observing and interviewing key informants in the newsrooms, I also identified and interviewed various leaders from different racial-ethnic communities. The point of these interviews was to help in determining what kind of job the newsrooms were doing in terms of covering issues important to people of color in the community. This process was obviously not all inclusive, but did provide me with a wealth of information to begin identifying some of the issues concerning news coverage. Although not a random survey, it provided much pertinent information. The purpose was not to try and compile profiles of the ethnic communities, but instead, utilize opinions of people in the community to help construct a critique of local news coverage. I was not to trying to represent these communities, or speak on behalf of these people, but instead give them an opportunity to critique local news operations. The goal was, to some extent, to try and see television news coverage through the eyes of the people who have traditionally been left on the outside, looking in. It is important to give audience members voice in a project like this, so that we do not forget that television viewers do not speak with one voice and are not just one large, unidentified mass of people. My motivation for doing this analysis is similar to why Fiske (1987) has found it important to study television audiences.

> Its value for us lies in its shift of emphasis away from textual and ideological construction of the subject to socially and historically situated people. It reminds us that actual people in actual situations watch and enjoy actual television programs. It acknowledges the differences between people despite their social construction, and pluralizes the meanings and pleasures that they find in television. It thus contradicts theories that stress the singularity of television's meanings and its reading subjects. (p. 63)

I began this process by identifying community groups that were active within the community. First, simply by watching and reading local news I was able to identify groups that were involved in local issues. This was often my starting point. I would then begin a process of networking, asking the people in these groups to recommend other groups. I tried to gather as much background information as possible about both groups and individuals before doing formalized interviews. Although I tried to select a wide spectrum of informants from different political and socio-economic backgrounds, I was in no way trying to construct any type of statistically representative sample. Instead, I was looking for a wide variety of opinion, in order to put together a varied critique of the local television news coverage. I interviewed tribal officials, government administrators, members of state legislatures, mayors, a newspaper columnist, a radio talk-show host, a host of a local-access cable television program, a federal civil rights administrator, a primary school teacher, a civil rights attorney, a historian working at a cultural center, grass roots organizers, a priest, a pastor, a director of an ethnic studies program, editors of local community newspapers, a physician, local business owners, and environmental activists. All of the people I interviewed said they were regular viewers of local television news, and many of them, at one time or another, had been closely connected to stories covered by local television news.

In all, 47 taped interviews were conducted with 50 people inside and outside of the news stations, of which all but one were conducted face-to-face. Another 34 less formal conversations took place over the phone and at different locations in and around Albuquerque and Honolulu. Twenty-three of the formal and 16 of the informal interviews took place in Hawai'i. Twenty-four formal interviews took place in New Mexico, 18 informal.

Station workers were promised a level of anonymity. I agreed not to identify the specific station studied, or the news worker themselves by name. Sources outside the stations were told they would be identified in the research by name. I felt that news workers might speak more openly with a level of anonymity, but that it was important for people reading this research to know exactly who the sources were that offered critiques of coverage.

I began each formal interview with the same list of eight questions, but allowed the interviewee to guide the content of the interview as much as possible. The eight questions were formed by information gathered from the review of literature. I almost always began with a general, open-ended question about television news coverage, and often the interviewee would continue on from there.

I would then ask follow-up questions about specific comments made. I was surprised that many of the interviewees had thought relatively extensively about local television coverage or lack thereof, and could articulate in some detail discontent with the amount and form of coverage their particular constituency had received.

I had little trouble setting up the interviews, because when I would mention that I wanted to talk with them about television news coverage, informants were often anxious to voice their opinions. These individuals had varied relationships with the television stations. Some were covered regularly and rated as excellent their relationships with the media; others had never been interviewed or even contacted by local news workers. At times, people I interviewed were both attracted and repelled by local television news. For example, one informant insisted the interview take place at the local television station. She requested a tour of the facility and wanted to meet the primary news anchor (a popular local celebrity) as part of her visit, yet her interview provided a scathing critique of the coverage that station and other local stations had provided of her community.

Another aspect of the relationship between television news operations and racial-ethnic communities is the fact that although viewers may have individual readings of things they see on television, this does not change an inherent power imbalance between those who own the television station, and those who do not have equal financial resources by which they might express their ideas to the community.

> In dealing with the institutional contexts in which ideologies are produced, one's attention must include consideration of inequities in the distribution of social resources. These inequities are not only important for determining who has access to means of cultural production; they also become problems with respect to social control that may result in attempted ideological resolutions. (Wuthnow, 1992, p. 123)

No matter how smaller, less powerful groups feel about news coverage, they generally will not have the resources to compete with multi-million dollar television stations, or broadcast chains. Wuthnow also points out that cultural producers often have a stake in maintaining their position, so that messages that would threaten their own continued well-being might not readily be presented. An example was found in Honolulu, one of my research sites, where there is currently a growing sovereignty movement. A scenario in which Hawai'i would no longer be part of the United States would be perceived as not beneficial for commercial television operations, therefore it was important to look at how the local news operation dealt with coverage of the sovereignty movement. A news operation may not be overt in behavior, such as in avoiding coverage completely, but there may exist more subtle effects, such as where the story is played within the newscast, or even what language and pictures are used to tell the story. Fiske (1987) wrote about how television gives preferred readings to messages that may continue to support the dominant *status quo*.

> Because television is an institutional art with a strong economic motive, this preferred reading will normally bear the dominant ideology, and the relation of any one subculture's reading to the preferred reading reproduces the relation of subculture to the dominant ideology. (p.117)

Others have also talked about social and cultural institutions' continued support of hegemony (Gerbner, 1972; Gitlin 1980, 1983; Tuchman, 1978b).

## ANALYSIS

Initial analysis took place in the field, even as data were gathered. After leaving the research sites and transcribing interviews and organizing field notes, I then began comparing the two sets of data, looking for recurring regularities to be sorted into categories for further analysis (Patton, 1980). As Huberman and Miles (1994) have explained:

> Most of these procedures call for the use of analytic induction. At the heart of analytic induction is the thesis that there are regularities to be found in the physical and social worlds. The theories or constructs that we derive express these regularities as precisely as possible. (p. 431)

These regularities have been classified into types and were checked to insure they share similar qualities. From this cross-case comparison, some conclusions emerged. These trends will need to be examined in light of existing theoretical frames to see if these data provide support for existing constructs about media. There may be the need to develop or build new theory to help explain and understand the data, as well.

Once certain regularities were identified, then came the job of weaving them together into a cogent narrative so readers could understand the general trends the researcher has identified.

> The ethnographer is not committed to "any old story," but wants to provide an account that communicates with the reader about the truth about the setting and the situation, as the ethnographer has come to understand it. For the ethnographer, the notion of validity does count, although it is acknowledged that other researchers at different times may come away with different interpretations. (Altheide & Johnson, 1994, p. 496)

The process of writing is also another step in the analytical process. Richardson (1994, p. 523) has talked about how writers also experience the act of discovery even as they attempt to put things down on paper. So even in the act of writing, more analysis and interpretation occur. Throughout this process, it was crucial to continue being reflective about the work. It was important to keep in mind a number of factors, including the relationship between what was observed and the larger cultural, historical, and organizational contexts within which the observations were made, the relationships among the observer, the observed, and the setting, and the issue of the representational style used by the writer in description and interpretation (Altheide & Johnson, 1994, p. 489).

# RATIONALE

A qualitative approach was chosen for several reasons. It seemed that to understand the process of news practice, a locally centered site was a logical choice. For it to be possible to look closely at news as a process, a qualitative approach allowed me to consider such factors as individual points of view and everyday social constraints. The goal was to produce a study that examined the emic, wherein one could find case-based examples that would serve to enrich our understanding of some trends that have already been identified on a more etic basis, through more traditional and positivist methodologies.

This is in many ways exploratory research. It does not fall within traditional definitions of anthropological ethnography, but ethnographic methods such as participant observation (albeit participating in a peripheral role) and in-depth interviewing were utilized. The incorporation of perspectives from people outside the newsroom in order to critique news practice, linked with the examination of certain texts, suggests a methodology drawing from a critical theory perspective. The combination of approaches, from my perspective, served to provide a dynamic synthesis of methodologies which seemed most appropriate to the questions at hand.

Because of the theoretical and methodological choices made before and during this research project, I aimed at providing description and hermeneutical understanding. Life as we know it is always bounded by certain constraints, such as current beliefs, cultural constructions, and historical circumstances. Therefore it may be most effective in a project such as this to provide description of conventions that may or may not support certain theoretical strands. As was discussed in the first chapter, hegemony and the theory of everyday racism seemed most pertinent to this researcher in looking at race-ethnicity and local news coverage. The goal, then, was to attempt to illuminate a social process in light of what was observed in comparison to these theoretical theses. As we continue our debates about post-modernism and research this seemed a prudent path, as suggested by scholars such as Geertz (1973), Agar (1986), and Clifford and Marcus (1986).

# References

Adler, P. A., & Adler, P. (1987). *Membership roles in field research.* Newbury Park, CA: Sage.

Adler, P. A., & Adler, P. (1994). Observational techniques. In N. K. Denzin & Y. S. Lincoln (Eds.), *Handbook of qualitative research* (pp. 377–392). Thousand Oaks, CA: Sage.

Agar, M. H. (1980). *The professional stranger: An informal introduction to ethnography.* Orlando, FL: Academic Press.

Altheide, D. L., & Johnson, J. M. (1994). Criteria for assessing interpretive validity in qualitative research. In N. K. Denzien & Y. S. Lincoln (Eds.), *Handbook of qualitative research.* Thousand Oaks, CA: Sage.

Altheide, D. L., & Rasmussen, P. K. (1976). Becoming news: A study of two newsrooms. *Sociology of Work and Occupations, 3,* 223–246.

Altschull, J. H. (1984). *Agents of power.* New York: Longman.

Appiah, K. A. (1995). Race. In F. Lentrichhia & T. McLaughlin (Eds.), *Critical terms for literary study* (2nd ed.). Chicago: University of Chicago Press.

Bagdikian, B. (1983). *The media monopoly.* Boston: Beacon.

Benedict, R. (1934). *Patterns of culture.* Boston: Houghton Mifflin.

Busterna, J. C. (1980). Ownership, CATV and expenditures for local television news. *Journalism Quarterly, 57,* 287–291.

Busterna, J. C. (1988). Television ownership effects on programming and idea diversity: Baseline data. *Journal of Media Economics, 1,* 63–74.

Carey, J. W. (1989). *Communication as culture.* Boston: Unwin Hyman.

Clifford, J., & Marcus, G. E. (Eds.). (1986). *Writing culture: The poetics and politics of ethnography.* Berkeley: University of California Press.

Dates, J. L., & Barlow, W. (1990). *Split image: African Americans in the mass media.* Washington, DC: Howard University Press.

Denzin, N. K., & Lincoln, Y. S. (1994). Introduction: Entering the field of qualitative research. In N. K. Denzin & Y. S. Lincoln (Eds.), *Handbook of qualitative research* (pp. 1–17). Thousand Oaks, CA: Sage.

Entman, R. M. (1989). *Democracy without citizens: Media and the decay of American politics.* Oxford: Oxford University Press.

Entman, R. M. (1990). Modern racism and the images of Blacks in local television news. *Critical Studies in Mass Communication, 7*, 332–345.

Entman, R. M. (1992). Blacks in the news: Television, modern racism and cultural change. *Journalism Quarterly, 69*(2), 341–361.

Essed, P. (1991). *Understanding everyday racism.* Newbury Park, CA: Sage.

Fine, G. D. (1993). Ten lies of ethnography: Moral dilemmas of field research. *Journal of Contemporary Ethnography, 22*, 267–294.

Fiske, J. (1987). *Television culture.* London: Routledge.

Geertz, C. (1973). *The interpretation of cultures.* New York: Basic Books.

Gerbner, G. (1972). Violence in television drama: Trends and symbolic function. In G. S. Comstock & E. A. Rubin (Eds.), *Television and social behavior, Vol. I: Media content and control* (pp. 28–187). Washington, DC: U.S. Government Printing Office.

Gitlin, T. (1980). *The whole world is watching.* Berkeley: University of California Press.

Gitlin, T. (1983). *Inside prime time.* New York: Pantheon.

Glazer, N., & Moynihan, D. P. (1968). *Beyond the melting pot.* Cambridge: MIT Press. (Original work published 1963)

Gray, H. (1987). Race relations as news. *American Behavioral Scientist, 30*, 381–396.

Gregory, D. (1994). *Geographical imaginations.* Oxford: Basil Blackwell.

Gutiérrez, F. (1980). *Latinos and the media in the United States: An overview.* Paper presented at the International Communication Association Conference.

Hall, S. (1977). Culture, media and the "ideological effect." In J. Curran, M. Gurevitch, & J. Wollacott (Eds.), *Mass communication and society.* London: Edward Arnold.

*Harvard Encyclopedia of American Ethnic Groups.* (1980.) (S. Thernstrom, Ed.) Cambridge, MA: Harvard University Press.

Heider, D. (1996). Completeness and exclusion in journalism ethics: An ethnographic case study. *Journal of Mass Media Ethics, 11*, 4–15.

Hodder, I. (1994). The interpretation of documents and material culture. In N. K. Denzin & Y. S. Lincoln (Eds.), *Handbook of qualitative research* (pp. 393–402). Thousand Oaks, CA: Sage.

Huberman, A. M., & Miles, M. B. (1994). Data management and analysis methods. In N. K. Denzien & Y. S. Lincoln (Eds.), *Handbook of qualitative research.* Thousand Oaks, CA: Sage.

Klaidman, S., & Beauchamp, T. L. (1987). *The virtuous journalist.* Oxford: Oxford University Press.

Lull, J. (1995). *Media, communication, culture: A global approach.* New York: Columbia University Press.

Lieberson, S., & Waters, M. C. (1988). *From many strands: Ethnic and racial groups in contemporary America.* New York: Russell Sage Foundation.

Martín-Barbero, J. (1987). *Communication, culture and hegemony: From the media to mediations.* London: Sage.

McManus, J. (1988). *An economic theory of news selection.* Paper presented at the annual conference for Association for Education in Journalism and Mass Communication, Portland, OR.

McManus, J. (1989). *Comparing an economic model of news selection with one based on professional norms in local television newscasts.* Paper presented at the annual conference of the Association for Education in Journalism and Mass Communication, Washington, DC.

Omi, M., & Winant, H. (1986). *Racial formation in the United States: From the 1960s to the 1980s*. New York: Routledge.

Papper, B., Gerhard, M., & Sharma, A. (1996). More women and minorities in broadcast news. *Communicator, 8*, 8–15.

Park, R. (1914). Racial assimilation in secondary groups. *American Journal of Sociology*, 607.

Patton, M. Q. (1980). *Qualitative evaluation and research methods*. Newbury Park, CA: Sage.

Pippert, W. G, (1989). *An ethics of news*. Washington, DC: Georgetown University Press.

Postman, N. (1985). *Amusing ourselves to death: Public discourse in an age of show business*. New York: Penguin.

Raveau, F. (1968). An outline of the role of color in adaptation. In J. H. Franklin (Ed.), *Color and race*. Boston: Houghton Mifflin

Richardson, L. (1994). Writing: A method of inquiry. In N. K. Denzin & Y. S. Lincoln (Eds.), *Handbook of qualitative research*. Thousand Oaks, CA: Sage.

Ringer, B. B., & Lawless, E. R. (1989). *Race-ethnicity and society*. New York: Routledge.

Sibley, D. (1995). *Geographies of exclusion*. London: Routledge.

Smythe, D. W. (1981). *Dependency road: Communications, capitalism, consciousness and Canada*. Norwood, NJ: Ablex.

Soloski, J. (1989). News reporting and professionalism: Some constraints on the reporting of the news. *Media, Culture and Society, 11*, 207–228.

Spradley, J. P. (1979). *The ethnographic interview*. Fort Worth, TX: Holt, Rinehart, & Winston.

Stone, V. (1988). *Pipelines and deadlines: Jobs held by minorities and women in broadcast news*. Paper presented at the annual conference of the Association for Education in Journalism and Mass Communication, Portland, OR.

Stone, V. (1993). Good news, bad news. *Communicator, 47*, 69.

Tuchman, G. (1978a). *Making news: A study in the construction of reality*. New York: The Free Press.

Tuchman, G. (1978b). Introduction: The symbolic annihilation of women by the mass media. In G. Tuchman, A. K. Daniels, & J. Benet (Eds.), *Hearth and home: Images of women in the mass media*. New York: Oxford University Press.

Turow, J. (1992). *Media systems in society: Understanding industries, strategies, and power*. White Plains, NY: Longman.

U.S. Commission on Civil Rights. (1977). *Window dressing on the set: Women and minorities in television*. Washington, DC: U.S. Government Printing Office.

U.S. Commission on Civil Rights. (1979). *Window dressing on the set: An update*. Washington, DC: U.S. Government Printing Office.

van Zoonen, L. (1988). Rethinking women and the news. *European Journal of Communication, 3*, 35–53.

Wax, M. L. (1977). On fieldworkers and those exposed to fieldwork. *Human Organization, 37*, 321–328.

Whyte, W. F. (1955). *Street corner society: The structure of an Italian slum*. Chicago: University of Illinois Press.

Wilson, C. C., & Gutiérrez, F. (1985). *Minorities and media: Diversity and the end of mass communication*. Beverly Hills, CA: Sage.

Wilson, C. C., & Gutiérrez, F. (1995). *Race, multiculturalism and the media.* Thousand Oaks, CA: Sage.

Winant, H. (1994). *Racial conditions: Politics, theory, comparisons.* Minneapolis: University of Minnesota Press.

Wuthnow, R. (1992). *Rediscovering the sacred: Perspectives on religion in contemporary society.* Grand Rapids, MI: William B. Eerdmans.

# Index